Calculations 5

Solutions

PUBLISHED BY THE PRESS SYNDICATE OF THE UNIVERSITY OF CAMBRIDGE
The Pitt Building, Trumpington Street, Cambridge, United Kingdom

CAMBRIDGE UNIVERSITY PRESS
The Edinburgh Building, Cambridge CB2 2RU, UK
40 West 20th Street, New York, NY 10011-4211, USA
10 Stamford Road, Oakleigh, VIC 3166, Australia
Ruiz de Alarcón 13, 28014 Madrid, Spain
Dock House, The Waterfront, Cape Town 8001, South Africa

http://www.cambridge.org

© Cambridge University Press 2001

First published 2001

Printed in the United Kingdom at the University Press, Cambridge

Typefaces Frutiger, Swift   *System* QuarkXPress 4.1®

A catalogue record for this book is available from the British Library

ISBN 0 521 79830 2 paperback

General editors for Cambridge Mathematics Direct
Sandy Cowling, Jane Crowden, Andrew King, Jeanette Mumford

Writing team for *Calculations 5*
Sandy Cowling, Pete Crawford, Jane Crowden, Claire Grigson, Gill Hatch, Andrew King, Mary Nathan, Kathryn Slowey, Allison Toogood, Cathy Tracy, Fay Turner

The writers and publishers would like to thank the many schools and individuals who trialled lessons for Cambridge Mathematics Direct.

NOTICE TO TEACHERS
The pages in this publication may be photocopied free of charge for classroom use within the school or institution which purchases the publication. Worksheets and photocopies of them remain in the copyright of Cambridge University Press and such photocopies may not be distributed or used in any way outside the purchasing institution. Written permission is necessary if you wish to store the material electronically.

Notes

Solutions to textbook and copymaster questions are listed under the title of the lesson in the teacher's handbook. Lessons are in the same order as in the teacher's handbook.

Solutions are written in different forms:
- Complete solutions are listed wherever it is useful.
- For open-ended questions and investigations, the possibilities are indicated through examples.

You can learn most about children's misconceptions by marking their work with them or discussing incorrect answers after marking.

Solutions may be photocopied (under the conditions detailed above).

Addition and subtraction

AS1.1 Checking addition

TB pages 5–6

★1 a 88 + 12 = 100   12 + 88 = 100
       100 − 12 = 88   100 − 88 = 12
    b 63 + 37 = 100   37 + 63 = 100
       100 − 37 = 63   100 − 63 = 37
    c 55 + 45 = 100   45 + 55 = 100
       100 − 45 = 55   100 − 55 = 45
    d 41 + 19 = 60   19 + 41 = 60
       60 − 19 = 41   60 − 41 = 19
    e 26 + 24 = 50   24 + 26 = 50
       50 − 24 = 26   50 − 26 = 24
    f 25 + 24 = 49   24 + 25 = 49
       49 − 24 = 25   49 − 25 = 24

A1 a 136 + 174 = 310   174 + 136 = 310
       310 − 174 = 136   310 − 136 = 174
    b 227 + 141 = 368   141 + 227 = 368
       368 − 141 = 227   368 − 227 = 141
    c 495 − 272 = 223   495 − 223 = 272
       223 + 272 = 495   272 + 223 = 495
    d 822 − 614 = 208   822 − 208 = 614
       208 + 614 = 822   614 + 208 = 822

A2 a 745 − 386 = 359   745 − 359 = 386
       359 + 386 = 745   386 + 359 = 745
    b 521 − 173 = 348   521 − 348 = 173
       348 + 173 = 521   173 + 348 = 521
    c 642 − 184 = 458   642 − 458 = 184
       458 + 184 = 642   184 + 458 = 642
    d 973 − 142 = 831   973 − 827 = 146
       831 + 142 = 973   146 + 827 = 973

B1 There are 21 possible pairs. For example:
    263 + 406 = 669
    Check: 669 − 263 = 406 or 669 − 406 = 263

B2 a 117 + 276 = 393 (wrong)
    b 313 + 319 = 632 (right)
    c 378 + 578 = 956 (wrong)
    d 364 + 263 = 627 (wrong)
    e 193 + 531 = 724 (right)
    f 587 + 435 = 1022 (wrong)

C1 Children's pairs totalling 1000, and subtraction checks

AS1.2 Splitting numbers to add

TB pages 7–8

A1 Children should show how they split the numbers to add, and give at least 2 ways.
    a 353 + 43 = **396**   b 246 + 41 = **287**
    c 762 + 36 = **798**   d 124 + 65 = **189**
    e 427 + 46 = **473**   f 354 + 27 = **381**

B1 Children should show how they split the numbers to add, and give at least 2 ways.
    a 337 + 8 = **345**   b 293 + 42 = **335**
    c 572 + 55 = **627**   d 446 + 76 = **522**
    e 819 + 93 = **912**   f 407 + 68 = **475**

B2 Children's additions shown in 2 different ways

C1 tennis balls: £3.48 + 75p = £4.23
    netballs: £4.85 + 75p = £5.60
    rackets: £7.49 + 47p = £7.96
    frisbees: £5.79 + 47p = £6.26
    bats: £6.24 + 47p = £6.71

CM 1

1   371 = 300 + 70 + 1
    634 = 600 + 30 + 4
    752 = 700 + 50 + 2
    246 = 200 + 40 + 6
    353 = 300 + 50 + 3
    174 = 100 + 70 + 4

2   370 + 20 = 300 + 70 + 20 = 300 + 90 = 390
    370 + 26 = 370 + 20 + 6 = 390 + 6 = 396
    630 + 20 = 600 + 30 + 20 = 600 + 50 = 650
    630 + 24 = 630 + 20 + 4 = 650 + 4 = 654
    750 + 30 = 700 + 50 + 30 = 700 + 80 = 780
    750 + 35 = 750 + 30 + 5 = 780 + 5 = 785
    752 + 35 = 750 + 2 + 35 = 785 + 2 = 787
    240 + 30 = 200 + 40 + 30 = 200 + 70 = 270
    240 + 32 = 240 + 30 + 2 = 270 + 2 = 272
    246 + 32 = 240 + 6 + 32 = 272 + 6 = 278

AS1.3 Calculating and recording HTU + HTU

TB pages 9–10

★1 Children should record the number sentence and the working in columns for 2 or 3 pairs:
    625 + 341 = 966   625 + 234 = 859
    625 + 153 = 778   625 + 130 = 755
    625 + 122 = 747   341 + 234 = 575
    341 + 153 = 494   341 + 130 = 471
    341 + 122 = 463   234 + 153 = 387
    234 + 130 = 364   234 + 122 = 356
    153 + 130 = 283   153 + 122 = 275
    130 + 122 = 252

A1 Children should show their working in columns.
Monday: 392
Tuesday: 503
Wednesday: 457
Thursday: 526
Friday: 653
Saturday: 913
Sunday: 774

B1 S & M: 197 + 109 = 306
S & H: 197 + 123 = 320
A & M: 155 + 109 = 264
A & H: 155 + 123 = 278
A & K: 155 + 134 = 289
A & Y: 155 + 144 = 299
Y & M: 144 + 109 = 253
Y & H: 144 + 123 = 267
Y & K: 144 + 134 = 278
K & M: 134 + 109 = 243
K & H: 134 + 123 = 257
H & M: 123 + 109 = 232
(The only pairs not possible are S & A, S & Y, S & K.)

C1 drinks   378 + 455 = 833
cards   473 + 217 + 168 = 858
rings   684 + 728 = 1412
sweets   715 + 268 + 355 = 1338

AS1.4 Starting with the thousands

TB pages 11–12

★1 Children should show their working in columns.
a 5300   b 7600
c 3900   d 9900
e 3723   f 5734
g 3450   h 7550
i 3773   j 6362

A1 There are 66 possible number pairs. Children should give a number sentence and working in columns for each of the 5 pairs chosen. For example:
a   1331
   + 6406
     7000
      700
       30
        7
     7737
   1331 + 6406 = 7737

b 6406 + 4283 = 10689 is the largest total.
c 1331 + 1552 = 2883 is the smallest total.
d 1331 + 3439 = 4770
   1331 + 2812 = 4143
   1331 + 3047 = 4378
   1331 + 2864 = 4195
   1331 + 2797 = 4128
   2458 + 1552 = 4010
   3439 + 1552 = 4991
   2812 + 1552 = 4364
   3047 + 1552 = 4599
   2864 + 1552 = 4416
   2797 + 1552 = 4349

B1 a 3284 + 1539 + 4168 = 8991
    1652 + 4316 + 5467 = 11322   3725 = 9693
    2934 + 5467 + 2461 = 10862
    The last row has the highest total.
b 3284 + 1652 + 2934 = 7870
   1539 + 4316 + 5467 = 11322
   4168 + 3725 + 2461 = 10354
   The middle column has the highest total.
c The first column has the lowest total.
d The first row has the total closest to 9000.

C1 Children total the numbers they make.

AS1.5 Carrying

TB pages 13–14

★1 Possible scores are:
138 + 245 = 383
138 + 354 = 492
138 + 516 = 654
245 + 354 = 599
245 + 516 = 761
354 + 516 = 870

A1   754   691   887
     + 1975   + 1868   + 2037
       2729   2559   2924
        1 1   1 1   1 1

        1358   1463   1286
     + 1467   + 1595   + 856
       2825   3058   2142
        1 1   1 1   1 1 1

B1 a 1071 − 384 = 687 or 1071 − 697 = 374
       384 + 697 = 1081
    b 1357 − 584 = 773 or 1357 − 773 = 584
       The addition is correct.

    c   2143 − 665 = 1478 or 2143 − 1478 = 665
         The addition is correct.
    d   1780 − 1229 = 551 or 1780 − 561 = 1219
         1229 + 561 = 1790
    e   4395 − 2419 = 1976 or 4395 − 1876 = 2519
         2419 + 1876 = 4295
    f   8075 − 4417 = 3658 or 8075 − 3658 = 4417
         The addition is correct.

C1   necklace + ring, 3310 points
       necklace + ring + medallion, 3775 points
       necklace + goblet, 3111 points
       necklace + goblet + medallion, 3576 points
       bangle + watch, 3615 points
       bangle + ring + medallion, 3328 points
       bangle + ring + goblet, 3600 points
       watch + ring + goblet, 3361 points
       watch + ring + medallion, 3089 points
       watch + ring + goblet + medallion, 3826 points

Homework suggestion

2374 + 465 = 2839
1927 + 465 = 2392
1927 + 737 = 2664
1927 + 936 = 2863
1688 + 465 = 2153
1688 + 737 = 2425
1688 + 936 = 2624

AS2.1 Using known subtraction facts

TB page 15

★1   a   7 − 5 = 2 so 70 − 50 = **20**
       b   10 − 4 = 6 so 100 − 40 = **60**
       c   13 − 8 = 5 so 130 − 80 = **50**
       d   22 − 6 = 16 so 220 − 60 = **160**

A1   a   15 − 8 = **7** so 150 − 80 = **70**
       b   27 − 15 = **12** so 270 − 150 = **120**
       c   49 − 26 = **23** so 490 − 260 = **230**
       d   54 − 18 = **36** so 5400 − 1800 = **3600**

A2   a   **44 − 16 = 28** so 440 − 160 = **280**
       b   **73 − 24 = 49** so 730 − 240 = **490**
       c   **57 − 39 = 18** so 570 − 390 = **180**
       d   **82 − 27 = 55** so 820 − 270 = **550**

A3   Children make up a number story for a sentence from A2.

C1   Children make up a number story for each subtraction sentence from 'Pick a sum'.

AS2.2 Using number pairs to 100

TB page 16

B1   a 600 − 536 = 64   b 900 − 817 = 83
       c 500 − 402 = 98   d 700 − 648 = 52
       e 800 − 776 = 24   f 400 − 312 = 88

B2   £77

B3   38 more children

B4   22 cm taller

B5   Calculator check:
       B1a 64 + 536 = 600   B1b 83 + 817 = 900
       B1c 98 + 402 = 500   B1d 52 + 648 = 700
       B1e 24 + 776 = 800   B1f 88 + 312 = 400
       B2   77 + 523 = 600   B3   38 + 362 = 400
       B4   22 + 178 = 200

C1   a   1000 − 973 = 27
          1000 − 873 = 127
          1000 − 773 = 227
          1000 − 673 = 327
          1000 − 573 = 427
          1000 − 473 = 527
          1000 − 373 = 627
          1000 − 273 = 727
          1000 − 173 = 827
          1000 − 73 = 927
    b   Each time you take away 100 less, the answer gets 100 greater.

C2   a   1000 − 973 = 27
          1000 − 963 = 37
          1000 − 953 = 47
          1000 − 943 = 57
          1000 − 933 = 67
          1000 − 923 = 77
          1000 − 913 = 87
          1000 − 903 = 97
          1000 − 893 = 107
    b   Each time you take away 10 less, the answer gets 10 greater.

C3   Children suggest patterns, for example:
       Each time you take away 1 less, the answer gets 1 greater.
       If you make the numbers on the left of the = sign 10 times bigger, the answer is 10 times greater.

AS2.3 Counting up HTU – HTU

TB page 17

A1 a   541
       − 264
       ─────
         36   to reach 300
        200   to reach 500
         41   to reach 541
       ─────
        277

    b   473
       − 158
       ─────
         42   to reach 200
        200   to reach 400
         73   to reach 473
       ─────
        315

    c   739
       − 488
       ─────
         12   to reach 500
        200   to reach 700
         39   to reach 739
       ─────
        251

    d   625
       − 279
       ─────
         21   to reach 300
        300   to reach 600
         25   to reach 625
       ─────
        346

B1 A   520
       − 387
       ─────
         13   to reach 400
        100   to reach 500
         20   to reach 520
       ─────
        (133)

    D   732
       − 499
       ─────
          1   to reach 500
        200   to reach 700
         32   to reach 732
       ─────
        (233)

    E   912
       − 689
       ─────
         11   to reach 700
        200   to reach 900
         12   to reach 912
       ─────
        (223)

    F   531
       − 189
       ─────
         11   to reach 200
        300   to reach 500
         31   to reach 531
       ─────
        (342)

    H   630
       − 279
       ─────
         21   to reach 300
        300   to reach 600
         30   to reach 630
       ─────
        (351)

    I   918
       − 388
       ─────
         12   to reach 400
        500   to reach 900
         18   to reach 918
       ─────
        (530)

    N   606
       − 391
       ─────
          9   to reach 400
        200   to reach 600
          6   to reach 606
       ─────
        (215)

    R   827
       − 496
       ─────
          4   to reach 500
        300   to reach 800
         27   to reach 827
       ─────
        (331)

    S   425
       − 176
       ─────
         24   to reach 200
        200   to reach 400
         25   to reach 425
       ─────
        (249)

    T   807
       − 292
       ─────
          8   to reach 300
        500   to reach 800
          7   to reach 807
       ─────
        (515)

    U   432
       − 170
       ─────
         30   to reach 200
        200   to reach 400
         32   to reach 432
       ─────
        (262)

B2   The treasure is under the fir tree.

Homework suggestion

Challenge 1: 987 − 245 = 742
Challenge 2: 527 − 498 = 29 or
              824 − 795 = 29

AS2.4 Counting up and exchange

TB page 18

B1 a 532   400 + 120 + 12
       − 286   − 200 + 80 + 6
       ─────   ──────────────
        246   200 + 40 + 6

    b 744   600 + 140 + 4
       − 574   − 500 + 70 + 4
       ─────   ──────────────
        170   100 + 70 + 0

    c 693   600 + 80 + 13
       − 475   − 400 + 70 + 5
       ─────   ──────────────
        218   200 + 10 + 8

    d 925   800 + 110 + 15
       − 167   − 100 + 60 + 7
       ─────   ──────────────
        758   700 + 50 + 8

    e 807   700 + 100 + 7
       − 525   − 500 + 20 + 5
       ─────   ──────────────
        282   200 + 80 + 2

    f 731   700 + 20 + 11
       − 222   − 200 + 20 + 2
       ─────   ──────────────
        509   500 + 00 + 9

B2 a £6.26   £5 + 1.1 + 0.16
       − £2.68   − £2 + 0.6 + 0.08
       ──────   ─────────────────
        £3.58   £3 + 0.5 + 0.08

    b £8.17   £7 + 1.0 + 0.17
       − £5.39   − £5 + 0.3 + 0.09
       ──────   ─────────────────
        £2.78   £2 + 0.7 + 0.08

    c £21.30   £20 + 1.2 + 0.10
       − £8.65   − £8 + 0.6 + 0.05
       ──────   ─────────────────
        £12.65   £12 + 0.6 + 0.05

CM 6

1   734   700 + 30 + 4   600 + 120 + 14
    − 268 − 200 + 60 + 8 − 200 + 60 + 08
                           ────────────────
                           400 + 60 + 6   466

2   851   800 + 50 + 1   700 + 140 + 11
    − 174 − 100 + 70 + 4 − 100 + 70 + 4
                           ────────────────
                           600 + 70 + 7   677

3   647   600 + 40 + 7   500 + 130 + 17
    − 369 − 300 + 60 + 9 − 300 + 60 + 9
                           ────────────────
                           200 + 70 + 8   278

4   903   900 + 00 + 3   800 + 90 + 13
    − 488 − 400 + 80 + 8 − 400 + 80 + 8
                           ────────────────
                           400 + 10 + 5   415

CM 7

1   267   200 + 60 + 7
    − 134 − 100 + 30 + 4
    ───── ──────────────
     133   100 + 30 + 3

2   486   400 + 80 + 6
    − 253 − 200 + 50 + 3
    ───── ──────────────
     233   200 + 30 + 3

3   692   600 + 80 + 12
    − 345 − 300 + 40 + 5
    ───── ───────────────
     347   300 + 40 + 7

4   761   700 + 50 + 11
    − 248 − 200 + 40 + 8
    ───── ───────────────
     513   500 + 10 + 3

5   568   400 + 160 + 8
    − 273 − 200 + 70 + 3
    ───── ────────────────
     295   200 + 90 + 5

AS3.1 Add or subtract and adjust

TB page 19

A1 a 162 + 95 = 162 + 100 − 5 = 257
    b 458 + 199 = 458 + 200 − 1 = 657
    c 367 + 497 = 367 + 500 − 3 = 864
    d 621 + 69 = 621 + 70 − 1 = 690
    e 153 + 38 = 153 + 40 − 2 = 191
    f 218 + 997 = 218 + 1000 − 3 = 1215

A2 a 723 − 99 = 723 − 100 + 1 = 624
    b 614 − 199 = 614 − 200 + 1 = 415
    c 386 − 299 = 386 − 300 + 1 = 87
    d 841 − 95 = 841 − 100 + 5 = 746
    e 187 − 69 = 187 − 70 + 1 = 118
    f 762 − 396 = 762 − 400 + 4 = 366

B1 a 60   b 840   c 1440
    d 780   e 1720   f 13 600

B2 a £7755   b £6870   c £8925

B3 a £14 441   b £15 156   c £16 990

C1 a Children find 3 pairs of numbers greater than 200 and with a difference of 97. For example, 201 & 298, 203 & 300, 1200 & 1297.
    b 198 & 6, 196 & 4, 194 & 2, 192 & 0
       If children include negative numbers there is an infinite number of pairs: 190 & −2, 188 & −4, ...

Homework suggestion

89, 188, 287, 386, 485, 584, 683, 782, 881, 980
The hundreds digit increases by 1 and the units digit decreases by 1 each time.

1079, 1178, 1277, 1376, 1475, 1574, ...
When you continue the next number is 1079, then the hundreds digit increases by 1 and the units digit decreases by 1 each time until the units digit becomes 0 once more.

If you add 98, the hundreds digit increases by 1 and the units digit decreases by 2 each time.

If you subtract 99, the hundreds digit decreases by 1 and the units digit increases by 1 each time.

AS3.2 Find the difference

CM10

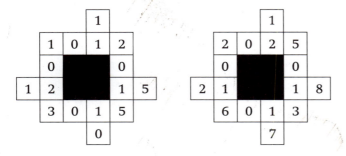

2 arrangements are possible for each diagram. The second is the reflection of the one given here in the diagonal going down from left to right.

AS3.3 Add too much and take away

TB pages 20–21

A1 a 12
    b 367
       + 188
       ─────
         567   367 add 200
       − 12   take away 12
       ─────
         555

A2 a 14
    b 235
       + 486
       ─────
         735   235 add 500
       − 14   take away 14
       ─────
         721

A3 a 0.22
    b 4.65
       + 2.78
       ─────
         7.65   4.65 add 3
       − 0.22   take away 0.22
       ─────
         7.43

B1 a, b Children find 5 of the following:
    348 + 192 = 540   562 + 387 = 949
    348 + 277 = 625   562 + 679 = 1241
    348 + 387 = 735   634 + 192 = 826
    348 + 679 = 1027   634 + 277 = 911
    427 + 192 = 619   634 + 387 = 1021
    427 + 277 = 704   634 + 679 = 1313
    427 + 387 = 814   851 + 192 = 1043
    427 + 679 = 1106   851 + 277 = 1128
    562 + 192 = 754   851 + 387 = 1238
    562 + 277 = 839   851 + 679 = 1530

    c 634 and 277 give the total closest to 900.

B2 a 8.5   b 17.2   c 23.6
    d 24.5   e £11.13   f £6.23

AS3.4 Take away too much and add back

TB page 22

B1 a 532 − 285 = 532 − 300 + 15 = 247
    b 648 − 179 = 648 − 200 + 21 = 469
    c 851 − 383 = 851 − 400 + 17 = 468

B2 a £367 − £185 = £367 − £200 + £15 = £182
    b £9.35 − £7.89 = £9.35 − £8 + £0.11 = £1.46
    c £7.45 − £3.89 = £7.45 − £4 + £0.11 = £3.56
    d £8.65 − £6.88 = £8.65 − £7 + £0.12 = £1.77
    e £5.75 − £3.85 = £5.75 − £4 + £0.15 = £1.90
    f £9.55 − £6.89 = £9.55 − £7 + £0.11 = £2.66

AS4.1 Adding and subtracting multiples of 10

TB pages 23–24

A1 a 650 + 350 = 1000   b 850 + 150 = 1000
    c 1000 − 250 = 750   d 1000 − 450 = 550

A2 a 160 + 130 = 290   b 420 + 150 = 570
    c 380 + 120 = 500   d 560 + 190 = 750
    e 240 + 260 = 500   f 340 − 140 = 200
    g 570 − 210 = 360   h 460 − 230 = 230
    i 930 − 150 = 780   j 810 − 360 = 450

A3 a 650 ml   b 850 g   c 260 ices

B1 a 710 − 470 = 240   b 430 + 370 = 800
    c 480 + 250 = 730   d 230 + 310 = 540
    e 650 − 380 = 270   f 930 − 580 = 350

B2 a Sian's house to the pond, to the PO:
       930 m
    b 1310 m
    c Bus stop to the PO, to the pond, to home

C1 3 routes from:
    Home to the PO, to the bus stop, by the
    road to the church, to the pond and home,
    2580 m
    Home to the PO, to the bus stop, by the
    path to the church, to the pond and home,
    2890 m
    Home to the pond, to the PO, to the bus
    stop, by the road to the church, to the pond
    and home, 2560 m
    Home to the pond, to the PO, to the bus
    stop, by the path to the church, to the pond
    and home, 2870 m
    Home to the pond, to the church, by the
    path to the bus stop, by the road to the
    church, to the pond and home, 2930 m
    Other routes involve going in the opposite
    direction, or going over some parts twice.

CM 13

1   16 + 13 = 16 + 10 + 3 = **29**
    16 tens + 13 tens = **29 tens**
    So 160 + 130 = **290**

2   34 − 14 = 34 − 10 − 4 = **20**
    34 tens − 14 tens = **20 tens**
    So 340 − 140 = **200**

3   27 + 14 = 41 so 270 + 140 = **410**

4   75 − 16 = 59 so 750 − 160 = **590**

CM 14

1

+	130	250
420	550	670
280	410	530

+	140	210
350	490	560
150	290	360

2, 3 Children's own puzzles and solutions

AS4.2 Adding 3-digit multiples of 100

TB pages 25–26

B1 a 2000. For example,
       7 + 4 = 11, 11 + 9 = 20, so 7 hundreds +
       4 hundreds + 9 hundreds = 20 hundreds
    b 500. For example,
       300 + 900 = 1200.
       12 + 5 = 17, so 1200 + 500 = 1700
    c 900. For example,
       8 + 6 = 14, and 14 + 9 = 23.
       So 800 + 600 + 900 = 2300
    d 800. For example,
       5 + 8 = 13, and 21 − 13 = 8.
       So 500 + 800 + 800 = 2100

B2 a 300 + 700 + 900 = 1900
       288 + 676 + 940 ≈ 1900
    b 500 + 900 + 100 = 1500
       456 + 860 + 147 ≈ 1500
    c 900 − 200 = 700. 937 − 184 ≈ 700
    d 900 − 300 = 600. 884 − 276 ≈ 600

B3

600	100	800
700	500	300
200	900	400

B4 a 400
    b 3 out of:
       900 + 300 + 300
       900 + 600 + 0
       800 + 700 + 0
       800 + 400 + 300
       700 + 500 + 300
       700 + 400 + 400
       600 + 600 + 300
       600 + 500 + 400
       500 + 500 + 500

Extension activity

There are 4 possible answers with 3 numbers:
900 + 800 + 300, 900 + 700 + 400, 900 + 600 + 500,
800 + 700 + 500

There are 10 possible answers with 4 numbers:
900 + 800 + 200 + 100, 900 + 700 + 300 + 100,
900 + 600 + 400 + 100, 900 + 600 + 300 + 200,
900 + 500 + 400 + 200, 800 + 700 + 400 + 100,
800 + 700 + 300 + 200, 800 + 600 + 500 + 100,
800 + 600 + 400 + 200, 800 + 500 + 400 + 300

CM 15

Children need to think about which combinations make 1000.
The only triples are 100, 200, 700; 100, 300, 600; 100, 400, 500; 200, 300, 500.
100 appears in 3 of the 4 winning combinations, so put 100 in the centre, with 200, 300 and 500 along one side and 700 diagonally opposite 200, 600 opposite 300, and 400 diagonally opposite 500.

AS4.3 Addition and subtraction with multiples of 100

TB page 27

B1   a   400 + 862 = **1262**   b   937 + 500 = **1437**
     c   1276 − 300 = **976**   d   1582 − 700 = **882**
     e   751 + 800 = **1551**   f   700 + 946 = **1646**
     g   1890 − 900 = **990**   h   1157 − 600 = **557**

B2   a   800. The tens and units have not changed, so the difference is a multiple of 100.
     b   500. The tens and units have not changed, so the difference is a multiple of 100.
     c   600. The tens and units have not changed, so the number is a multiple of 100.
     d   1265. The number being taken away is a multiple of 100, so the tens and units will be the same as in the answer.
     e   335. The number being added is a multiple of 100, so the tens and units will be the same as in the answer.
     f   600. The tens and units have not changed, so the difference is a multiple of 100.

B3   a   £510   b   £110
     c   £470   d   £500

CM 17

1   500 + 200 = **500**   500 + 400 = **900**
     560 + 200 = **760**   500 + 420 = **920**
     600 + 300 = **900**   700 + 500 = **1200**
     685 + 300 = **985**   714 + 500 = **1214**

2   900 − 200 = **700**   1200 − 300 = **900**
     940 − 200 = **740**   1270 − 300 = **970**
     800 − 500 = **300**   1600 − 700 = **900**
     867 − 500 = **367**   1694 − 700 = **994**

CM 18

1   1381 − **500** = 881
     697 + 400 = **1097**
     300 + **1108** = 1408
     700 + 614 = 1314

2   Children's own clues and completed cross number

Homework suggestion

There are 8 possible number sentences:
981 + 500 = 1481   1276 + 500 = 1776
981 + 700 = 1681   1276 + 700 = 1976
981 − 500 = 481   1276 − 500 = 776
981 − 700 = 281   1276 − 700 = 576
If a 3rd number was placed in box A, there would be another 4 sentences.

AS5.1 Adding several numbers 1

TB pages 28–29

A1   a   36   b   38   c   300
     d   250   e   150   f   90

B1   a   £1.03   b   £1.41   c   £1.46

B2   ping pong ball, score sheet and whistle: 38p + 21p + 41p = £1

B3   a   Children pick 3 numbers and find the total.
     b   Largest total: 50 + 60 + 70 = 180
     c   Smallest total: 11 + 13 + 19 = 43

C1   Children choose 13 numbers such that the sum of the lowest 3 is between 75 and 100, and the sum of the highest 3 is between 175 and 200. For example:
20, 25, 35, 40, 42, 45, 48, 50, 55, 58, 60, 65, 70

AS5.2 Recording in columns

TB pages 30–31

A1   a   324 + 558 = 882 (carry 1)   b   567 + 115 = 682 (carry 1)
     c   376 + 272 = 648 (carry 1)   d   514 + 398 = 912 (carry 1 1)

A2   £426

B1 a 2369   b 4884
       + 3956   + 3623
       ──────   ──────
        6325   8507
        1 1 1   1 1

    c 3649   d 5483
       + 1538   + 2689
       ──────   ──────
        5187   8172
        1   1   1 1 1

B2 a 1571 g   b 1373 g
    c 1498 g   d 3875 g or 3.875 kg

C1 a 2436 + 1587 = 4023
       These are not winning numbers.
    b 1000 and any number from 3501 to 3999,
       1001 and any number from 3500 to 3998,
       1002 and any number from 3499 to 3997,
       and so on.

AS5.3 Adding several numbers 2

TB pages 32–33

B1 a   67   b   8
        1024   6354
        5293   207
       + 852   + 2507
       ──────   ──────
        7236   9076
        1 2 1   1   2

    c   1301   d   45
         810   657
          12   4925
       + 8000   + 390
       ──────   ──────
       10123   6017
           1   2 2 1

B2 a If they buy a tape deck they have £301
       left. For example, they could buy an
       amplifier, a radio, 9 CDs and 4 cassettes
       (with £1 left over).
    b If they buy the CD player they have £151
       left. For example, they could buy an
       amplifier, 2 CDs and 2 cassettes.
    c A CD player and tape deck cost £548.

B3   £16.50
        £9.00
       £12.25
        £5.00
       ──────
       £42.75
          2

C1 a 17 942p   b £179.42
    c 8870p or £88.70. This is just less than
       half the total.

AS6.1 Using a calculator

TB pages 34–35

A1 a Estimate: 300 + 400 + 200 = 900
       Calculator: 827
       Answer: 827 cm of ribbon altogether
    b Estimate: 620 − 590 = 30
       Calculator: 34
       Answer: 34 records left
    c Estimate: 8000 − 400 − 600 − 900 = 6100
       or 400 + 600 + 900 = 1900
           8000 − 1900 = 6100
       Calculator: 6139
       Answer: 6139 g of rice is left.
    d Estimate: 400 + 800 = 1200
       Calculator: 1138
       Answer: They weigh 1138 g altogether.

A2 Check of answers to A1

B1 a £44   b 714 people   c 1950 m
    d No. He has saved £90.32. He needs £9.17
       more.

B2 Mrs Green wins the ghetto blaster.
    Cho wins the tennis racket.
    Beth wins the wine.

C1 a 791   b 368
    c Children choose their own starting
       number. The answer should be 525 less
       than the starting number.
    d Children's own number chains
    e Children's own chain with the same
       start and end number

AS6.2 Decomposition ThHTU − ThHTU

TB pages 36–37

A1 a   4596   3000 + 1500 + 90 + 6
       − 2713   2000 + 700 + 10 + 3
       ──────   ─────────────────────
        1883   1000 + 800 + 80 + 3

    b   8257   7000 + 1200 + 50 + 7
       − 3647   3000 + 600 + 40 + 7
       ──────   ─────────────────────
        4610   4000 + 600 + 10 + 0

    c   3682   3000 + 600 + 70 + 12
       − 1455   1000 + 400 + 50 + 5
       ──────   ─────────────────────
        2227   2000 + 200 + 20 + 7

    d   7618   7000 + 500 + 110 + 8
       − 5294   5000 + 200 + 90 + 4
       ──────   ─────────────────────
        2324   2000 + 300 + 20 + 4

B1 a $\overset{5\ 1\ 7\ 1}{\cancel{6}\cancel{3}\cancel{8}4}$ b $\overset{6\ 11\ 1}{\cancel{7}\cancel{2}4\cancel{6}}$
       -2619 -4883
       3765 2363

    c $\overset{2\ 11\ 1}{\cancel{3}\cancel{2}2\cancel{7}}$ d $\overset{1\ 15\ 1}{5\cancel{2}6\cancel{4}}$
       -1634 -2188
       1593 3076

B2 a 558 g   b 758 g   c 925 g

C1 a $\overset{5\ 1}{8\cancel{6}\cancel{3}}$ b $\overset{2\ 1}{67\cancel{3}\cancel{0}}$
       -245 -4219
       618 2511

    c $\overset{4\ 1\ 8\ 1}{\cancel{5}4\cancel{9}\cancel{2}}$
       -2977
       2515

C2 a 624 – 140, 625 – 141, 626 – 142,
       627 – 143, 628 – 144, 629 – 145

    b 8065 – 4580, 8066 – 4581, 8067 – 4582,
       8068 – 4583, 8069 – 4584
       8165 – 4680, 8166 – 4681, 8167 – 4682,
       8168 – 4683, 8169 – 4684
       8265 – 4780, 8266 – 4781, 8267 – 4782,
       8268 – 4783, 8269 – 4784
       8365 – 4880, 8366 – 4881, 8367 – 4882,
       8368 – 4883, 8369 – 4884
       8465 – 4980, 8466 – 4981, 8467 – 4982,
       8468 – 4983, 8469 – 4984

AS6.3 Decomposition with decimals

TB page 38

★1 a   364   300 + 50 + 14
       − 128   100 + 20 + 8
        236   200 + 30 + 6

    b   5725   5000 + 600 + 120 + 5
       − 2491   2000 + 400 + 90 + 1
        3234   3000 + 200 + 30 + 4

    c   3681   3000 + 600 + 70 + 11
       − 457   400 + 50 + 7
        3224   3000 + 200 + 20 + 4

    d   63.7   60 + 2 + 1.7
       − 10.8   10 + 0 + 0.8
        52.9   50 + 2 + 0.9

A1 a $\overset{6\ 15\ 1}{2\cancel{7}\cancel{6}\cancel{2}}$ b $\overset{1\ 1}{\cancel{2}\cancel{8}.6}$
       -385 -19.4
       2377 9.2

    c $\overset{3\ 12\ 11\ 1}{\cancel{4}\cancel{3}\cancel{2}.\cancel{2}3}$ d $\overset{5\ 1\ 7\ 1}{\cancel{6}\cancel{1}\cancel{8}.0}$
       -87.6 -24.2
       344.67 593.8

    e $\overset{2\ 9\ 10\ 1}{\cancel{3}\cancel{0}\cancel{1}.2}$ f $\overset{2\ 13\ 1\ 5\ 1}{\cancel{3}4\cancel{5}\cancel{6}.0}$
       -56.8 -674.1
       244.4 2781.9

C1 a,b Children's choice of 5 pairs of numbers
         and the difference between them
    c   2280 and 9.4 give the largest difference,
         2270.6.
    d   68.7 and 76.5 give the smallest
         difference, 7.80.
    e   Any one of the numbers and a number
         150 more or less than it, for example,
         534 and 684.

CM 20

1   15.2 → [10.8] → 26 → [11.3] → 37.3 → [32.5]
    → 69.8 → [41.3] → 111.1 → [106.7] → 217.8
    → [415.2] → 633 → [117.2] → 750.2

2   735

AS7.1 Doubling decimals

TB pages 39–40

A1 a 0.2   b 0.6
    c 0.9   d 0.3

A2 a 0.4 m   b 0.2 m
    c 0.8 m   d 0.7 m
    e 0.9 m   f 0.6 m

B1 a 1.8 m + **0.2** m = 2 m
    b **7.3** m + 0.7 m = 8 m
    c 0.4 m + **5.6** m = 6 m
    d 13.2 m + **0.8** m = 14 m

B2 a 2.6 m   b 3.6 m
    c 13 m   d 21.4 m

B3 a 2.6 + 2.6 = 5.2
    b 2.6 + 2.7 = 5.3
    c 2.6 + 2.5 = 5.1
    d For example: The answer to b is 0.1 more
       than the answer to a, and the answer to
       c is 0.1 less than the answer to a.
       Or: You find the answer to a by doubling
       2.6; you find the answer to b and c by
       doubling 2.6 and adjusting by 0.1.

C1	a	7.2 m	b	3.6 m
	c	8.4 m	d	10.6 m
	e	18.2 m	f	4.8 m

C2 Children's 10 'near doubles' questions, for example:
3.6 m + 3.7 m = 7.3 m

AS7.2 Adding and subtracting decimals

TB page 41

A1 1.5 + 8.5 = 10, 6.9 + 3.1 = 10, 4.4 + 5.6 = 10,
3.2 + 6.8 = 10

A2 Children give 4 of the 17 possible pairs:
8.5 + 6.9 = 15.4, 8.5 + 6.8 = 15.3,
8.5 + 5.9 = 14.4, 8.5 + 5.6 = 14.1,
8.5 + 4.4 = 12.9, 8.5 + 3.2 = 11.7,
8.5 + 3.1 = 11.6, 6.9 + 6.8 = 13.7,
6.9 + 5.9 = 12.8, 6.9 + 5.6 = 12.5,
6.9 + 4.4 = 11.3, 6.9 + 3.2 = 10.1,
6.8 + 5.9 = 12.7, 6.8 + 5.6 = 12.4,
6.8 + 4.4 = 11.2, 5.9 + 5.6 = 11.5,
5.9 + 4.4 = 10.3

B1 a 7.5   b 5.6   c 4.7
    d 4.6   e 10.1   f 4.8

B2 a 7.5 − 4.9 = 2.6 or 7.5 − 2.6 = 4.9
    b 5.6 + 5.2 = 10.8
    c 4.7 + 2.5 = 7.2
    d 4.6 − 3.2 = 1.4 or 4.6 − 1.4 = 3.2
    e 10.1 − 1.4 = 8.7 or 10.1 − 8.7 = 1.4
    f 4.8 + 4.3 = 9.1

B3 a 6.25 + 3.12 = 9.37
    b 8.67 + 3.45 = 12.12

B4 5.26 m − 1.43 m = 3.83 m

B5 1.17 m − 0.89 m = 0.28 m

AS7.3 Adding and subtracting decimals in columns

TB page 42

★1 a   3.2   b   4.8
       + 5.4   + 3.7
         8.6   8.5

    c   7.6   d   6.3
       − 2.1   − 1.6
         5.5   4.7

A1 a   2.14   b   5.75
       + 3.62   + 6.19
         5.76   11.94

    c   8.84   d   9.63
       − 4.34   − 6.35
         4.50   3.28

A2 a   £2.64   b   £5.81
       + £6.63   − £1.62
         £9.27   £4.19

    c   £8.87   d   £7.46
       + £6.54   − £6.68
        £15.41   £0.78

C1 a Combined length   b Extra space

De & Co: 3.12 m + 1.38 m = 4.50 m   0 m
P & Co: 2.51 m + 1.38 m = 3.89 m   0.61 m
P & Dr: 2.51 m + 1.76 m = 4.27 m   0.23 m
P & Tr: 2.51 m + 1.86 m = 4.37 m   0.13 m
O & Co: 2.12 m + 1.38 m = 3.50 m   1 m
O & Dr: 2.12 m + 1.76 m = 3.88 m   0.62 m
O & Tr: 2.12 m + 1.86 m = 3.98 m   0.52 m
Tr & Co: 1.86 m + 1.38 m = 3.24 m   1.26 m
Tr & Dr: 1.86 m + 1.76 m = 3.62 m   0.88 m
Dr & Co: 1.76 m + 1.38 m = 3.14 m   1.36 m

AS7.4 Solving decimal problems

TB pages 43–44

★1 a   £7.54   b   £4.57
       + £1.25   + £2.29
         £8.79   £6.86

    c   £6.34   d   £8.63
       − £2.12   − £2.48
         £4.22   £6.15

A1 a a pot of coffee
       It is £0.46 or 46p more than a pot of tea.
       It is £0.70 or 70p more than a cola.
       It is £0.97 or 97p more than orange squash.
    b salmon & cucumber
       It is 28p more than the tuna & cucumber sandwich.
       It is 36p more than the ham & mustard sandwich.
       It is 58p more than the egg & cress sandwich.
    c Children's choice of sandwich and drink
       The most expensive is coffee and salmon sandwich, £4.28; change 22p.
       The cheapest is squash and egg sandwich, £2.73, change £1.77.

    d   Children's choice of drink, sandwich, fruit and cake. There is enough money to buy every combination. The most expensive is coffee, salmon sandwich, fruit and muffin, costing £6.20, leaving 5p.

B1   a   Children's choice of 3 items to buy and their total cost
    b   Cara bought the mug, the pen and the pencil sharpener.
    c   Children's choice of 5 items to buy and their total cost
    d   £14.50
    e   £29.35

C1   82.05 m

C2   maiasaura 3.7 m
       baryonyx 3.59 m
       albertosaurus 3.29 m
       triceratops 3.08 m
       tuojiangosaurus 1.79 m
       iguanodon 1.6 m

Multiplication and division

MD1.1 Which way round?

TB page 45

B1   a $12 \div 6 = 2$ $6 \div 12 = 0.5$
    b $28 \div 7 = 4$ $4 \div 28 = 0.1428$
    c $48 \div 6 = 8$ $6 \div 48 = 0.125$
    d $70 \div 7 = 10$ $7 \div 70 = 0.1$
    e $35 \div 7 = 5$ $7 \div 35 = 0.2$
    f $900 \div 10 = 90$ $10 \div 900 = 0.0111$
    g   The answer to the second division is a decimal fraction less than 1.
    h   For example, I changed the order of the numbers in a division, and got different answers.

C1   For example:
    a $7 \times 6 = 42$
    b $70 \times 6 = 420$
    c $9 \times 6 = 54$
    d $90 \times 6 = 540$
    e $50 \times 6 = 300$
    f $500 \times 6 = 3000$
    g   There are
        $420 + 42 + 540 + 54 + 300 + 3000$ eggs
        $= 3000 + 1200 + 150 + 6 = 4356$ eggs

C2   Children's orders for eggs

CM 23

1   $3 \times 4 = 12$ so $4 \times 3 = 12$
    $9 \times 2 = 18$ so $2 \times 9 = 18$
    $7 \times 5 = 35$ so $5 \times 7 = 35$
    $8 \times 6 = 48$ so $6 \times 8 = 48$
    $9 \times 3 = 27$ so $3 \times 9 = 27$
    $7 \times 4 = 28$ so $4 \times 7 = 28$

2   four fives: **20**
    2 lots of 7: **14**
    5 times 6: **30**

3   $8 \times 3 = 24$
    $6 \times 7 = 42$
    $10 \times 10 = 100$

4   10 multiplied by 2: **20**
    7 multiplied by 3: **21**
    9 multiplied by 4: **36**

5   $3 \times 6 = 18$
    $9 \times 5 = 45$
    $4 \times 6 = 24$

6   8×2 and 2×8
    9×10 and 10×9
    70×4 and 4×70
    5×3 and 3×5

MD1.2 Grouping and sharing

TB page 46

B1 Class 1
2 groups of 9   9 groups of 2
3 groups of 6   6 groups of 3

Class 2
3 groups of 9   9 groups of 3

Class 3
5 groups of 5

Class 4
2 groups of 15   15 groups of 2
3 groups of 10   10 groups of 3
5 groups of 6   6 groups of 5

Class 6
2 groups of 10   10 groups of 2
4 groups of 5   5 groups of 4

B2 There are 144 children.
2 groups of 72   72 groups of 2
3 groups of 48   48 groups of 3
4 groups of 36   36 groups of 4
6 groups of 24   24 groups of 6
8 groups of 18   18 groups of 8
9 groups of 16   16 groups of 9
12 groups of 12

C1 a small, 6 sets; medium, 12 sets;
       large, 24 sets
    b For example, each box has twice as
       many sets as the smaller box.
    c 48 sets
    d 384 pencils

C2 If there were 6 colours in each box there
    would be: small, 4 sets; medium, 8 sets;
    large, 16 sets; bumper, 32 sets.
    Again, each box has twice as many sets as
    the box before it.

CM 24

$30 \div 3$	30 shared between 3	10 each
$24 \div 2$	24 shared between 2	12 each
$36 \div 4$	36 shared between 4	9 each
$36 \div 6$	36 shared between 6	6 each
$40 \div 4$	40 shared between 4	10 each
$42 \div 7$	42 shared between 7	6 each

$27 \div 9$ How many groups of 9
can I take from 27?   3 groups

$42 \div 21$ How many groups of 21
can I take from 42?   2 groups

$30 \div 10$ How many groups of 10
can I take from 30?   3 groups

$33 \div 11$ How many groups of 11
can I take from 33?   3 groups

CM 25

1 a 3   b 6   c 9   d 6
   e 13 f 5   g 7   h 9

2 a 5   b 5   c 2   d 3
   e 4   f 7   g 3   h 4

MD1.3 Multiply and divide

TB page 47

A1 Children complete CM 26.

A2 Children make up division word problems
and check their partner's problems.

B1 a $36 \div 4 = 9$ b $18 \div 3 = 7$
       $4 \times 9 = 36$ $3 \times 7 = 21$
       right   wrong

    c $11 \times 5 = 55$ d $31 \times 3 = 39$
       $55 \div 11 = 5$ $39 \div 3 = 13$
       right   wrong

    e $44 \div 6 = 7$ f $44 \times 2 = 84$
       $6 \times 7 = 42$ $84 \div 2 = 42$
       wrong   wrong

    g $100 \div 5 = 19$ h $39 \div 13 = 3$
       $5 \times 19 = 95$ $13 \times 3 = 39$
       wrong   right

    i $19 \times 4 = 89$
       $89 \div 4 = 22 \text{ r } 1$
       wrong

B2 a $9 \times 8 = 72$ b $8 \times 7 = 56$
       $72 \div 9 = 8$ $56 \div 8 = 7$
       $72 \div 8 = 9$ $56 \div 7 = 8$

    c $9 \times 6 = 54$ d $15 \times 4 = 60$
       $54 \div 9 = 6$ $60 \div 15 = 4$
       $54 \div 6 = 9$ $60 \div 4 = 15$

    e $3 \times 21 = 63$ f $20 \times 8 = 160$
       $63 \div 3 = 21$ $160 \div 8 = 20$
       $63 \div 21 = 3$ $160 \div 20 = 8$

    g $25 \times 5 = 125$ h $26 \times 8 = 208$
       $125 \div 25 = 5$ $208 \div 26 = 8$
       $125 \div 5 = 25$ $208 \div 8 = 26$

C1 Children make up addition, subtraction,
multiplication and division word problems,
and check their partner's problems.

CM 26

6 ÷ 6 = **1**	24 ÷ 8 = **3**	70 ÷ 7 = **10**
36 ÷ 6 = **6**	72 ÷ 8 = **9**	56 ÷ 7 = **8**
60 ÷ 6 = **10**	40 ÷ 8 = **5**	7 ÷ 7 = **1**
12 ÷ 6 = **2**	80 ÷ 8 = **10**	63 ÷ 7 = **9**
24 ÷ 6 = **4**	32 ÷ 8 = **4**	21 ÷ 7 = **3**
54 ÷ 6 = **9**	48 ÷ 8 = **6**	42 ÷ 7 = **6**
18 ÷ 6 = **3**	8 ÷ 8 = **1**	35 ÷ 7 = **5**
30 ÷ 6 = **5**	16 ÷ 8 = **2**	49 ÷ 7 = **7**
48 ÷ 6 = **8**	56 ÷ 8 = **7**	14 ÷ 7 = **2**
42 ÷ 6 = **7**	64 ÷ 8 = **8**	28 ÷ 7 = **4**

MD1.4 Using factors to multiply

TB page 48

A1   a   3, 8   b   3, 9   c   2, 8   d   6, 8

A2 $5 \times 16 = 5 \times (2 \times 8)$
$= (5 \times 2) \times 8$
$= 10 \times 8$
$= \mathbf{80}$

$27 \times 2 = (9 \times 3) \times 2$
$= 9 \times (3 \times 2)$
$= 9 \times 6$
$= \mathbf{54}$

$3 \times 24 = 3 \times (3 \times 8)$
$= (3 \times 3) \times 8$
$= 9 \times 8$
$= \mathbf{72}$

$48 \times 5 = (6 \times 8) \times 5$
$= 6 \times (8 \times 5)$
$= 6 \times 40$
$= \mathbf{240}$

B1   a $12 \times 6 = (2 \times 6) \times 6$
$= 2 \times (6 \times 6)$
$= 2 \times 36$
$= \mathbf{72}$

b $3 \times 14 = 3 \times (7 \times 2)$
$= (3 \times 7) \times 2$
$= 21 \times 2$
$= \mathbf{42}$

c $24 \times 5 = (6 \times 4) \times 5$
$= 6 \times (4 \times 5)$
$= 6 \times 20$
$= \mathbf{120}$

d $13 \times 30 = 13 \times (3 \times 10)$
$= (13 \times 3) \times 10$
$= 39 \times 10$
$= \mathbf{390}$

e $15 \times 18 = 15 \times (2 \times 9)$
$= (15 \times 2) \times 9$
$= 30 \times 9$
$= \mathbf{270}$

f $25 \times 16 = 25 \times (4 \times 4)$
$= (25 \times 4) \times 4$
$= 100 \times 4$
$= \mathbf{400}$

B2   Children play 'Fast factors'.

C1   For example

$14 \times 19 = (14 \times 20) - 14$

$14 \times 22 = (14 \times 20) + 28$

$14 \times 25 = 7 \times 50$

$19 \times 22 = 20 \times 22 - 22$

$19 \times 25 = 20 \times 25 - 25$

$22 \times 25 = 11 \times 50$

MD2.1 Multiplying multiples of 10 and 100

TB page 49

B1 5×30 km = 150 km

B2 $8 \times £40 = £320$

B3 $4 \times 300 = 1200$ pennies

B4 8×500 cm = 4000 cm
4000 cm = 40 m

B5 $8 \times £800 = £6400$

B6 $8 \times £600 = £4800$

B7   £3.60 ÷ 40p = 360p ÷ 40p = 9, so 9 weeks

C1   When you multiply a multiple of 10 or 100 by a multiple of 10, you can just multiply the non-zero digits together then add all the zeros on, e.g. $50 \times 50 = \mathbf{2500}$

CM 28

1	60	2	80	3	80
4	150	5	180	6	200
7	420	8	400	9	360
10	480	11	490	12	800
13	800	14	1200	15	2500
16	2100	17	2400	18	4000
19	4900	20	5400	21	5600
22	20	23	60	24	70
25	3	26	7	27	9
28	50	29	9	30	80

MD2.3 Using a grid to record HTU × U

TB pages 50–51

★1 a $24 \times 4 =$

×	20	4
4	80	16

= 80 + 16 = 96

b $33 \times 5 =$

×	30	3
5	150	15

= 150 + 15 = 165

c $48 \times 3 =$

×	40	8
3	120	24

= 120 + 24 = 144

d $27 \times 6 =$

×	20	7
6	120	42

= 120 + 42 = 162

e $112 \times 3 =$

×	100	10	2
3	300	30	6

= 300 + 30 + 6 = 336

f $103 \times 4 =$

×	100	0	3
4	400	0	12

= 400 + 0 + 12 = 412

B1 a $195 \times 3 = 585$ aliens
    b $195 \times 7 = 1365$ aliens

B2 a $345 \times 6 = 2070$ chocolate bars
    b $345 \times 4 = 1380$ chocolate bars

B3 a $406 \times 8 = 3248$ days
    b $406 \times 5 = 2030$ days

C1 $456 \times 2 = 912$
    a $912 \times 4 = 3648$ m
    b $912 \times 7 = 6384$ m

C2 a $955 \times 2 = 1910$ litres
    b $955 \times 6 = 5730$ litres

C3 Children's own HTU × U word problems

CM 30

With the following bold multiplications inserted, the solutions are:

1 **325 × 3** is approximately $300 \times 3 = 900$

×	300	20	5
3	900	60	15

= 900 + 60 + 15 = 975

2 **136 × 6** is approximately $150 \times 5 = 750$

×	100	30	6
6	600	180	36

= 600 + 180 + 36 = 816

3 **423 × 8** is approximately $400 \times 10 = 4000$

×	400	20	3
8	3200	160	24

= 3200 + 160 + 24 = 3384

4 **574 × 6** is approximately $600 \times 5 = 3000$

×	500	70	4
6	3000	420	24

= 3000 + 420 + 24 = 3444

Note: The approximations given are just examples. Other reasonable approximations are equally acceptable.

MD2.4 Using columns

TB pages 52–53

★1 a
```
    2 3
  ×   4
    8 0
  + 1 2
    9 2
```

b
```
      4 5
    ×   5
    2 0 0
  +   2 5
    2 2 5
```

c
```
    6 3
  ×   3
  1 8 0
  +   9
  1 8 9
```

d
```
    5 2
  ×   7
  3 5 0
  + 1 4
  3 6 4
```

e
```
    6 7
  ×   8
  4 8 0
  +  5 6
  5 3 6
   1
```

f
```
    8 6
  ×   6
  4 8 0
  +  3 6
  5 1 6
   1
```

A1 a
```
    3 4 2
  ×     3
    9 0 0
    1 2 0
  +     6
  1 0 2 6
     1
```

b
```
    5 0 3
  ×     6
  3 0 0 0
        0
  +   1 8
  3 0 1 8
```

c
```
    3 8 4
  ×     4
  1 2 0 0
    3 2 0
  +   1 6
  1 5 3 6
```

d
```
    4 6 3
  ×     8
  3 2 0 0
    4 8 0
  +   2 4
  3 7 0 4
     1
```

e
```
    7 2 8
  ×     5
  3 5 0 0
    1 0 0
  +   4 0
  3 6 4 0
```

f
```
    5 9 2
  ×     7
  3 5 0 0
    6 3 0
  +   1 4
  4 1 4 4
     1
```

B1 a Children's own HTU × U product made using 4 digit cards, e.g. 3, 0, 7, 5 can be used as 305×7

    b Children use columns to find the answer to their product in part a

c Children find other possible HTU × U products for their digit cards
With 4 non-zero digits there are 24 possible products. If zero is included there are 12 non-trivial products.

B2 Children do B1 again

B3 a Children's own multiplication for which 900 × 4 = 3600 could be an estimate
b Children's own word problem to match their multiplication in part a
c Children find the answer to their multiplication in part a

B4 Children repeat B3 for the approximation 250 × 10 = 2500

C1 a
```
    1 4 5
  ×     5
  -------
    7 2 5
    2 2
```
b
```
    6 5 7
  ×     3
  -------
  1 9 7 1
    1 1 2
```
c
```
    4 2 6
  ×     4
  -------
  1 7 0 4
    1 1 2
```

C2 Children's own HTU × U multiplications

MD3.1 Division and fractions

CM 33

1 27: 3 × 9 = 27, 9 × 3 = 27, 27 ÷ 3 = 9, 27 ÷ 9 = 3
28: 4 × 7 = 28, 7 × 4 = 28, 28 ÷ 7 = 4, 28 ÷ 4 = 7
48: 6 × 8 = 48, 8 × 6 = 48, 48 ÷ 6 = 8, 48 ÷ 8 = 6
72: 8 × 9 = 72, 9 × 8 = 72, 72 ÷ 8 = 9, 72 ÷ 9 = 8

2 Children write 4 divisions for each given answer, for example
3: 6 ÷ 2 = 3
6: 36 ÷ 6 = 6
8: 72 ÷ 9 = 8

Homework suggestion

You can find $\frac{1}{4}$ but not $\frac{1}{8}$ of 4, 12, 20, 28, 36, 44, ...
You can find $\frac{1}{3}$ but not $\frac{1}{6}$ of 3, 9, 15, 21, 27, 33, ...

MD3.2 Writing remainders as fractions

TB page 54

A1 Children do CM 34.

A2 $25 \div 2 = 12\frac{1}{2}$
$46 \div 5 = 9 \text{ r } 1$
$82 \div 9 = 9\frac{1}{9}$
$49 \div 8 = 6\frac{1}{8}$
$57 \div 8 = 7\frac{1}{8}$
$73 \div 8 = 9\frac{1}{8}$

B1
	Number of bars	Number of aliens	How many each?
a	13	3	$4\frac{1}{3}$
b	26	5	$5\frac{1}{5}$
c	36	7	$5\frac{1}{7}$
d	49	6	$8\frac{1}{6}$
e	57	8	$7\frac{1}{8}$
f	64	9	$7\frac{1}{8}$ $7\frac{1}{9}$
g	71	10	$7\frac{1}{10}$

B2 Children's problems using the numbers from B1 a, b, c and d

C1 Children's problems using the numbers from B1 e, f and g

C2 Children's own division problems with mixed number answers

CM 34

1

Input	Output 1	Output 2
4 × 7 = 28	28 ÷ 7 = 4	28 ÷ 4 = 7
9 × 6 = 54	54 ÷ 6 = 9	54 ÷ 9 = 6
7 × 8 = 56	56 ÷ 8 = 7	56 ÷ 7 = 8
5 × 9 = 45	45 ÷ 9 = 5	45 ÷ 5 = 9
7 × 7 = 49	49 ÷ 7 = 7	49 ÷ 7 = 7
8 × 9 = 72	72 ÷ 9 = 8	72 ÷ 8 = 9
9 × 7 = 63	63 ÷ 7 = 9	63 ÷ 9 = 7
9 × 9 = 81	81 ÷ 9 = 9	81 ÷ 9 = 9
5 × 7 = 35	35 ÷ 7 = 5	35 ÷ 5 = 7
6 × 8 = 48	48 ÷ 8 = 6	48 ÷ 6 = 8

2 The following are correct:
$19 \div 3 = 6\frac{1}{3}$
$16 \div 5 = 3\frac{1}{5}$
$29 \div 4 = 7\frac{1}{4}$
$64 \div 9 = 7 \text{ r } 1$
$50 \div 7 = 7\frac{1}{7}$
$36 \div 5 = 7\frac{1}{5}$

MD3.3 Writing remainders as decimal fractions

CM 35

1.
fraction	$\frac{1}{2}$	$\frac{1}{4}$	$\frac{2}{4}$	$\frac{3}{4}$
decimal fraction	0.5	0.25	0.5	0.75

2.
in	out
7	3.5
13	6.5
19	9.5

in	out
17	4.25
22	5.5
27	6.75

3.
fraction	$\frac{1}{5}$	$\frac{2}{5}$	$\frac{3}{5}$	$\frac{4}{5}$	$\frac{1}{10}$	$\frac{3}{10}$	$\frac{5}{10}$	$\frac{7}{10}$
decimal fraction	0.2	0.4	0.6	0.8	0.1	0.3	0.5	0.7

4.
in	out
21	4.2
42	8.4
54	10.8
38	7.6
50	10

in	out
41	4.1
23	2.3
85	8.5
92	9.2
78	7.8

5. a $\frac{1}{2}$, $\frac{2}{4}$ and $\frac{5}{10}$ match 0.5.
    b $\frac{1}{5}$ and $\frac{2}{10}$ match 0.2; $\frac{2}{5}$ and $\frac{4}{10}$ match 0.4;
       $\frac{3}{5}$ and $\frac{6}{10}$ match 0.6; $\frac{4}{5}$ and $\frac{8}{10}$ match 0.8.
    c $\frac{1}{20}$ = 0.05, $\frac{2}{20}$ = 0.1, $\frac{3}{20}$ = 0.15, ...

Homework suggestion

Cost	Number of pens	Cost of each pen
£4	2	£2
	4	£1
	5	£0.80 or 80p
	10	£0.40 or 40p
	20	£0.20 or 20p
£10	2	£5
	4	£2.50
	5	£2
	10	£1
	20	£0.50 or 50p
£3	2	£1.50
	4	£0.75 or 75p
	5	£0.60 or 60p
	10	£0.30 or 30p
	20	£0.15 or 15p

MD4.1 Using multiples for TU ÷ U
TB pages 55–56

B1 a 78 ÷ 6 = 9   too small
    b 84 ÷ 3 = 28   about the right size ✓
    c 92 ÷ 4 = 37   too big
    d 95 ÷ 5 = 27   too big
    e 87 ÷ 3 = 19   too small
    f 93 ÷ 8 = 12   about the right size

    b   84   f   93
       − 60   20 × 3   − 80   10 × 8
         ‾‾
         24   8 × 3   13   1 × 8 r 5

B2 A = 19   L = 15   F = 24   T = 16
    O = 13   S = 17   Y = 14   I = 18
    FLY. ALL IS LOST.

C1 a 9 packs with 2 stickers over
    b 15 packs with 2 stickers over
    c 11 packs with 4 stickers over
    d 23 packs
    e 18 packs with 2 stickers over
    f 13 packs with 1 sticker over

C2 Sally's mum puts 4 stickers in each pack.

CM 36

1   Multiples of 3: 30, 9, 21, 18, 36
    Multiples of 8: 80, 16, 32, 88
    Multiple of 3 and 8: 24

2   a 51 ÷ 3 between 10 and 20
             because 10 × 3 = 30 and 20 × 3 = 60
       84 ÷ 6 between 10 and 20
             because 10 × 6 = 60 and 20 × 6 = 120
       92 ÷ 4 between 20 and 30
             because 20 × 4 = 80 and 30 × 4 = 120
       84 ÷ 7 between 10 and 20
             because 10 × 7 = 70 and 20 × 7 = 140
       75 ÷ 3 between 20 and 30
             because 20 × 3 = 60 and 30 × 3 = 90
       85 ÷ 5 between 10 and 20
             because 10 × 5 = 50 and 20 × 5 = 100

    b 51 ÷ 3 = 17   51 − 30 = 21
       84 ÷ 6 = 14   84 − 60 = 24
       92 ÷ 4 = 23   92 − 80 = 12
       84 ÷ 7 = 12   84 − 70 = 14
       75 ÷ 3 = 25   75 − 60 = 15
       85 ÷ 5 = 17   85 − 50 = 35

Homework suggestion

96 ÷ 3 = 32	93 ÷ 6 = 15 r 3	63 ÷ 9 = 7
69 ÷ 3 = 23	39 ÷ 6 = 6 r 3	36 ÷ 9 = 4

Allowing repeats, you also get

99 ÷ 3 = 33	99 ÷ 6 = 16 r 3	99 ÷ 9 = 11
96 ÷ 6 = 16	96 ÷ 9 = 10 r 6	93 ÷ 3 = 31
93 ÷ 9 = 10 r 3	69 ÷ 6 = 11 r 3	69 ÷ 9 = 7 r 6
66 ÷ 3 = 22	66 ÷ 6 = 11	66 ÷ 9 = 7 r 3
63 ÷ 3 = 21	63 ÷ 6 = 10 r 3	39 ÷ 3 = 13
39 ÷ 9 = 4 r 3	36 ÷ 3 = 12	36 ÷ 6 = 6
33 ÷ 3 = 11	33 ÷ 6 = 5 r 3	33 ÷ 9 = 3 r 6

MD4.2 Using multiples for HTU ÷ U

CM 37

1.
 - 105 ÷ 7   between 10 and 20
 - 144 ÷ 8   between 10 and 20
 - 112 ÷ 4   between 20 and 30
 - 175 ÷ 5   greater than 30
 - 168 ÷ 7   between 20 and 30
 - 192 ÷ 6   greater than 30
 - 114 ÷ 3   greater than 30
 - 126 ÷ 9   between 10 and 20

2. For example:

```
   105              144              112
 -  70  10 × 7    -  80  10 × 8    -  80  20 × 4
    35   5 × 7       64   8 × 8       32   8 × 4
 105 ÷ 7 = 15    144 ÷ 8 = 18    112 ÷ 4 = 28
  15 × 7 = 105    18 × 8 = 144    28 × 4 = 112

   175              168              192
 - 150  30 × 5    - 140  20 × 7    - 180  30 × 6
    25   5 × 5       28   4 × 7       12   2 × 6
 175 ÷ 5 = 35    168 ÷ 7 = 24    192 ÷ 6 = 32
  35 × 5 = 175    24 × 7 = 168    32 × 6 = 192

   114              126
 -  90  30 × 3    -  90  10 × 9
    24   8 × 3       36   4 × 9
 114 ÷ 3 = 38    126 ÷ 9 = 14
  38 × 3 = 114    14 × 9 = 126
```

3,4 Children check that answers agree with approximations and then use a calculator to check with the inverse operation.

5.

	¹1	8	
²3	5		³1
	2		⁴2	4
		⁵3	8

CM 38

clue	approximate answer	my exact answer	checked
189 ÷ 7	between 20 and 30	27	
168 ÷ 8	between 20 and 30	21	
160 ÷ 5	between 30 and 40	32	
284 ÷ 4	between 70 and 80	71	
156 ÷ 6	between 20 and 30	26	
208 ÷ 4	between 50 and 60	52	
196 ÷ 7	between 20 and 30	28	
192 ÷ 6	between 30 and 40	32	
558 ÷ 9	between 60 and 70	62	
153 ÷ 9	between 10 and 20	17	
152 ÷ 8	between 10 and 20	19	
295 ÷ 5	between 50 and 60	59	
496 ÷ 8	between 60 and 70	62	

¹3		²2	7		³6
⁴2	⁵1			⁶3	2
		⁷7	⁸1		
⁹5			9		
9			¹⁰2	¹¹6	
	¹²5	2		¹³2	8

Homework suggestion

The following divisions are possible:

864 ÷ 2 = 432	846 ÷ 2 = 423
684 ÷ 2 = 342	648 ÷ 2 = 324
486 ÷ 2 = 243	468 ÷ 2 = 234
862 ÷ 4 = 215 r 2	826 ÷ 4 = 206 r 2
682 ÷ 4 = 170 r 2	628 ÷ 4 = 157
286 ÷ 4 = 71 r 2	268 ÷ 4 = 67
842 ÷ 6 = 140 r 2	824 ÷ 6 = 137 r 2
482 ÷ 6 = 80 r 2	428 ÷ 6 = 71 r 2
284 ÷ 6 = 47 r 2	248 ÷ 6 = 41 r 2
642 ÷ 8 = 80 r 2	624 ÷ 8 = 78
462 ÷ 8 = 57 r 6	426 ÷ 8 = 53 r 2
264 ÷ 8 = 33	246 ÷ 8 = 30 r 6

MD4.3 Short division (HTU ÷ U)

TB pages 57–58

A1
```
    a  3)72              b  5)95
        - 60   20 × 3        - 50   10 × 5
          12                   45
        - 12    4 × 3        - 45    9 × 5
           0                    0
       Answer 20 + 4 = 24   Answer 10 + 9 = 19
```

A2 a 108 ÷ 4. Approximately 25. Answer 27
  b 222 ÷ 6. Approximately 40. Answer 37
  c 288 ÷ 8. Approximately 40. Answer 36
  d 168 ÷ 7. Approximately 20. Answer 24

B1 50 cars (297 ÷ 6 = 49 r 3)

B2 40 tickets (317 ÷ 8 = 39 r 5)

B3 Everyone can have one. (28 × 9p = £2.52)

B4 31 children (217p ÷ 7p = 31)

B5 32 tables (317 ÷ 10 = 31 r 7)

C1 Children play 'Biggest quotient'.

MD5.1 Using closely related facts to multiply

Homework suggestion

The square numbers to 15 × 15 are:
1, 4, 9, 16, 25, 36, 49, 64, 81, 100, 121, 144, 169, 196, 225.

MD5.2 Multiplying multiples of 10 and 100

TB pages 59–60

A1 Children's own choice of multiplication fact, e.g. 6 × 4, used to make new facts, e.g. 60 × 4 = 240, 6 × 40 = 240, 60 × 40 = 2400, 600 × 4 = 2400, 6 × 400 = 2400, …

A2 Children do A1 again

A3 a 40 × 20 = **800**, 40 × 19 = **760**
  b 90 × 20 = **1800**, 90 × 21 = **1890**
  c 15 × 20 = **300**, 15 × 19 = **285**
  d 17 × 20 = **340**, 17 × 21 = **357**
  e 21 × 20 = **420**, 21 × 19 = **399**

A4 Any 5 out of:
  20 × 30 = 600 20 × 90 = 1800
  20 × 70 = 1400 2 × 800 = 1600
  19 × 30 = 570 19 × 90 = 1710
  19 × 70 = 1330 40 × 30 = 1200
  40 × 90 = 3600 40 × 70 = 2800
  40 × 22 = 880 60 × 30 = 1800
  60 × 70 = 4200 60 × 10 = 600
  60 × 22 = 1320 500 × 6 = 3000
  50 × 30 = 1500 50 × 90 = 4500
  50 × 70 = 3500 50 × 22 = 1100

B1 Children work as fast as they can and write down how many seconds they took
  a 320 b 2800
  c 8000 d 1000
  e 2700 f 10 000
  g 48 000 h 750

B2 Children time themselves again
  a 304 b 28 000
  c 800 d 10 000
  e 27 000 f 10 000
  g 48 000 h 735

B3 a Gemma could make 4 different guesses:
    20 × 600 = 12 000
    60 × 200 = 12 000
    30 × 400 = 12 000
    40 × 300 = 12 000
  b 20 × 600 = 12 000

B4 70 × 800 = 56 000 or 80 × 700 = 56 000

C1 6000, 8000, 12 000 and 18 000 can all be made from four _0 × _00 multiplications.

Homework suggestion

There are 23 possible products:
100 × 10 = 1000
200 × 10 = 2000 100 × 20 = 2000
300 × 10 = 3000 100 × 30 = 3000
400 × 10 = 4000 100 × 40 = 4000
500 × 10 = 5000 100 × 50 = 5000
600 × 10 = 6000 100 × 60 = 6000
700 × 10 = 7000 100 × 70 = 7000
800 × 10 = 8000 100 × 80 = 8000
900 × 10 = 9000 100 × 90 = 9000
200 × 30 = 6000 200 × 20 = 4000
200 × 40 = 8000 300 × 20 = 6000
300 × 30 = 9000 400 × 20 = 8000

MD5.3 Using a grid for TU × TU

TB page 61

B1 a 34 × 26 is approximately 30 × 30 = 900 (other appropriate approximations are acceptable)

×	30	4	
20	600	80	680
6	180	24	204
			884

  b 45 × 32 is approximately 50 × 30 = 1500

×	40	5	
30	1200	150	1350
2	80	10	90
			1440

  c 46 × 53 is approximately 50 × 50 = 2500

×	40	6	
50	2000	300	2300
3	120	18	138
			2438

B2 a

×	50	5
70	3500	350
3	150	15

3850
 165
4015

Children check against an approximate answer, e.g. 60 × 70 = 4200

b

×	70	4
30	2100	120
6	420	24

2220
 444
2664

Children check against an approximate answer, e.g. 70 × 40 = 2800

c

×	60	8
50	3000	400
9	540	72

3400
 612
4012

Children check against an approximate answer, e.g. 70 × 60 = 4200

B3 Children's own word problems that match the multiplications in B2

C1 a 25 × 32   b 84 × 46

C2 Children's own grids with the numbers being multiplied missing

CM 39

With the calculations 14 × 15, 18 × 13, 14 × 26, 23 × 17, 28 × 24 and 32 × 27 filled in, the solutions are:

1 14 × 15 is approximately 10 × 20 = 200

×	10	4
10	100	40
5	50	20

140
 70
210

2 18 × 13 is approximately 20 × 10 = 200

×	10	8
10	100	80
3	30	24

180
 54
234

3 14 × 26 is approximately 10 × 30 = 300

×	10	4
20	200	80
6	60	24

280
 84
364

4 23 × 17 is approximately 20 × 20 = 400

×	20	3
10	200	30
7	140	21

230
 161
391

5 28 × 24 is approximately 30 × 20 = 600

×	20	8
20	400	160
4	80	32

560
 112
672

6 32 × 27 is approximately 30 × 30 = 900

×	30	2
20	600	40
7	210	14

640
 224
864

Other reasonable approximations are equally acceptable.

MD5.4 Using columns for TU × TU

TB pages 62–63

A1 a
$\quad\quad$ 32 $\quad\quad\quad\quad\quad$ 32
$\quad\quad$ × 3 $\quad\quad\quad\quad$ × 30
$\quad\quad$ 96 $\quad\quad\quad\quad\quad$ 960

b
$\quad\quad$ 42 $\quad\quad\quad\quad\quad$ 42
$\quad\quad$ × 4 $\quad\quad\quad\quad$ × 40
$\quad\quad$ 168 $\quad\quad\quad\quad$ 1680

c
$\quad\quad$ 17 $\quad\quad\quad\quad\quad$ 17
$\quad\quad$ × 5 $\quad\quad\quad\quad$ × 50
$\quad\quad$ 85 $\quad\quad\quad\quad\quad$ 850
$\quad\quad\quad$ 3 $\quad\quad\quad\quad\quad\quad\quad$ 3

d
$\quad\quad$ 68 $\quad\quad\quad\quad\quad$ 68
$\quad\quad$ × 4 $\quad\quad\quad\quad$ × 40
$\quad\quad$ 272 $\quad\quad\quad\quad$ 2720
$\quad\quad\quad$ 3 $\quad\quad\quad\quad\quad\quad\quad$ 3

A2 a $\quad$ 41 $\quad\quad\quad$ b $\quad$ 55
$\quad\quad\quad$ × 20 $\quad\quad\quad\quad\quad$ × 30
$\quad\quad\quad$ 820 $\quad\quad\quad\quad$ 1650
$\quad\quad\quad\quad\quad\quad\quad\quad\quad\quad\quad\quad$ 1

c $\quad$ 72
$\quad$ × 40
$\quad$ 2880

B1 a
$\quad\quad$ 24 $\quad\quad\quad\quad$ 24 $\quad\quad\quad\quad$ 24
$\quad\quad$ × 20 $\quad\quad\quad$ × 3 $\quad\quad\quad$ × 23
$\quad\quad$ 480 $\quad\quad\quad$ 72 $\quad\quad\quad$ 480
$\quad\quad\quad\quad\quad\quad\quad\quad$ 1 $\quad\quad\quad\quad\quad$ 72
$\quad\quad\quad\quad\quad\quad\quad\quad\quad\quad\quad\quad\quad$ 552

b
$\quad\quad$ 17 $\quad\quad\quad\quad$ 17 $\quad\quad\quad\quad$ 17
$\quad\quad$ × 30 $\quad\quad\quad$ × 5 $\quad\quad\quad$ × 35
$\quad\quad$ 510 $\quad\quad\quad$ 85 $\quad\quad\quad$ 510
$\quad\quad\quad$ 2 $\quad\quad\quad\quad\quad$ 3 $\quad\quad\quad\quad\quad$ 85
$\quad\quad\quad\quad\quad\quad\quad\quad\quad\quad\quad\quad\quad$ 595

c
$\quad\quad$ 38 $\quad\quad\quad\quad$ 38 $\quad\quad\quad\quad$ 38
$\quad\quad$ × 20 $\quad\quad\quad$ × 7 $\quad\quad\quad$ × 27
$\quad\quad$ 760 $\quad\quad\quad$ 266 $\quad\quad$ 760
$\quad\quad\quad$ 1 $\quad\quad\quad\quad\quad$ 5 $\quad\quad\quad\quad$ 266
$\quad\quad\quad\quad\quad\quad\quad\quad\quad\quad\quad\quad\quad$ 1026

| | | d | 56
× 40
2240
  2 | 56
× 8
448
  4 | 56
× 48
2240
448
2688 |

B2	a	Estimate: 60 × 20 = 1200

62
× 24
1240   62 × 20
 248   62 × 4
1488

b Estimate: 80 × 40 = 3200

79
× 43
3160   79 × 40
 237   79 × 3
3397

B3 a

74
× 36
2220   74 × 30
 444   74 × 6
2664

b

83
× 45
3320   83 × 40
 415   83 × 5
3735

c

67
× 44
2680   67 × 40
 268   67 × 4
2948

d

93
× 67
5580   93 × 60
 651   93 × 7
6231

C1 Children play '2-digit challenge', randomly picking 2-digit numbers to multiply

MD6.1 Using doubling and halving

TB pages 64–65

A1 Children double four randomly chosen 2-digit numbers,
e.g. 56 × 2 = (50 × 2) + (6 × 2)
= 100 + 12
= 112

A2 a 7 × 6 = **42** so 14 × 6 = **84**
b 9 × 3 = **27** so 18 × 3 = **54**
c 9 × 7 = **63** so 18 × 7 = **126**
d 7 × 8 = **56** so 14 × 8 = **112**

A3 a 14 × 9 = double (7 × 9) = double 63 = 126
b 5 × 18 = double (5 × 9) = double 45 = 90
c 16 × 6 = double (8 × 6) = double 48 = 96
d 8 × 22 = double (8 × 11) = double 88 = 176

B1 a 5 × 8 = **10** × 4 = **40**
b 14 × 5 = **7** × 10 = **70**
c 6 × 15 = **3** × 30 = **90**
d 15 × 18 = 30 × **9** = **270**

B2 a 92 × 50 = 46 × 100 = 4600
b 43 × 20 = 86 × 10 = 860
c 128 × 5 = 64 × 10 = 640
d 66 × 15 = 33 × 30 = 990
e × 20 is the same as double, then × 10
× 5 is the same as halve, then × 10
× 15 is the same as halve, then × 30

C1 a 18 → 9 → 24 → 12 → 6 → 3 → 18
All the numbers in the chain are multiples of 3.
b Children investigate different chains with starting numbers above 40. There are only 5 truly different chains, repeating on 16, 18, 20, 28 or 30.

C2 Children investigate longer number chains. There are only 3 truly different chains, repeating on 4, 20 and 100.

Homework suggestion

Numbers that end in 50 end in 00 when doubled.
Numbers that end in 25 end in 50 when doubled.
Numbers that end in 5 end in 0 when doubled.

MD6.2 Which way to multiply?

TB pages 66

★1 a 12 × 2 = 24 so 12 × 4 = **48**
b 18 × 2 = 36 so 18 × 4 = **72**
c 25 × 4 = **100**
d 23 × 4 = **92**

★2 a 8 × 10 = 80 so 8 × 5 = **40**
b 14 × 10 = 140 so 14 × 5 = **70**
c 25 × 5 = **125**
d 28 × 5 = **140**

★3 a 15 × 3 = 45 so 15 × 6 = **90**
b 21 × 3 = 63 so 21 × 6 = **126**
c 25 × 6 = **150**
d 33 × 6 = **198**

A1 Children play 'Hit the target'

CM 40

'Jackpot 500' with 59, 25, 43, 62, 46, 18, 78, 19, 37 and 21 written in:
Multiplying by 3, the closest you can get is 501 using 59, 62 and 46.
Multiplying by 4, it is possible to get within 4, e.g. $(4 \times 21) + (4 \times 25) + (4 \times 78) = 496$.
Multiplying by 5, it is possible to get within 5, e.g. $(5 \times 18) + (5 \times 46) + (5 \times 37) = 505$.

'Jackpot 1000' with 68, 47, 16, 35, 79, 64, 54, 53, 17 and 26 written in:
It is possible to reach 1000, e.g. multiplying by 5: $(5 \times 68) + (5 \times 79) + (5 \times 53) = 1000$.

MD6.3 Short multiplication: HTU × U

Homework suggestion

There are 2 ways to score 0:
$497 \times 2 = 994$
$479 \times 2 = 958$

There are 7 ways to score 1:
$249 \times 7 = 1743$
$279 \times 4 = 1116$
$297 \times 4 = 1188$
$749 \times 2 = 1498$
$794 \times 2 = 1588$
$947 \times 2 = 1894$
$974 \times 2 = 1948$

There are 4 ways to score 2:
$247 \times 9 = 2223$
$274 \times 9 = 2466$
$294 \times 7 = 2058$
$729 \times 4 = 2916$

There are 6 ways to score 3:
$427 \times 9 = 3843$
$429 \times 7 = 3003$
$492 \times 7 = 3444$
$792 \times 4 = 3168$
$927 \times 4 = 3708$
$972 \times 4 = 3888$

There is 1 way to score 4:
$472 \times 9 = 4248$

There are 4 ways to score 6:
$724 \times 9 = 6516$
$742 \times 9 = 6678$
$924 \times 7 = 6468$
$942 \times 7 = 6594$

MD7.1 Using a calculator to divide

TB pages 67–68

A1 a £4.63   b £7.60   c £8.05
    d £30.20   e £65   f £15.10

A2 a 9.26   b 3.7
    c 6.03   d 10.01

A3 a £8   b £44
    c £19   d £12

B1 a about £6 ÷ 4 = £1.50
    b about £14 ÷ 4 = £3.50
    c about £30 ÷ 5 = £6
    d about £9 ÷ 9 = £1
    e about £3 ÷ 10 = 30p
    f about £3 ÷ 3 = £1

B2 a £1.45   b £3.40   c £5.60
    d 95p   e 35p   f 91p

C1 a about £30 ÷ 10 = £3, exactly £4.02
    b about £100 ÷ 10 = £10, exactly £14.80
    c about £45 ÷ 3 = £15, exactly £13.79

C2 a 23.3333...
    b between £23 and £24

MD7.2 Short division with remainders: HTU ÷ U (1)

TB pages 69–70

A1 Children do CM 44.

A2 a
```
      5 7
  3 ) 1 7 1
      1 5
        2 1
```
b
```
      4 1
  6 ) 2 4 6
      2 4
        0 6
```
c
```
      1 2 9
  5 ) 6 4 5
      5
      1 4
      1 0
        4 5
```
d
```
      2 1 4
  4 ) 8 5 6
      8
      0 5
        4
        1 6
```

A3
```
        2 7
    6 ) 1 6 2
        1 2
          4 2
```
So 27 rows of hens.

A4   Children's own division word problems

B1   a
```
       3 7
   6 ) 2 2 2
       1 8
         4 2
```
b
```
         4 7
   9 ) 4 2 3
       3 6
         6 3
```
c
```
       1 8 8
   5 ) 9 4 0
       5
       4 4
       4 0
           4 0
             4 0
```
d
```
       2 8 2
   3 ) 8 4 6
       6
       2 4
       2 4
           0 6
```
e
```
       1 5 4  r 1
   6 ) 9 2 5
       6
       3 2
       3 0
         2 5
         2 4
             1
```
f
```
         4 4  r 1
   9 ) 3 9 7
       3 6
         3 7
         3 6
             1
```
g
```
       1 2 1  r 4
   5 ) 6 0 9
       5
       1 0
       1 0
           0 9
             5
             4
```
h
```
       1 5 6  r 2
   3 ) 4 7 0
       3
       1 7
       1 5
           2 0
           1 8
               2
```

B2
```
         5 4  r 2
   6 ) 3 2 6
       3 0
         2 6
         2 4
             2
```
There were 6 – 2 = 4 empty spaces.

B3
```
         2 6  r 6
   9 ) 2 4 0
       1 8
         6 0
         5 4
             6
```
It takes 27 journeys.

C1   Children find the underlined missing digits:
  a   <u>182</u> ÷ 5 = 36 r 2
  b   342 ÷ <u>7</u> = 48 r <u>6</u>
  c   <u>162</u> ÷ <u>7</u> = 23 r 1

CM 44

With 268 ÷ 4, 384 ÷ 6, 468 ÷ 9 and 516 ÷ 6 written on, the solutions are:

1
```
         6 7
   4 ) 2 6 8
       2 4
         2 8
```
2
```
         6 4
   6 ) 3 8 4
       3 6
         2 4
```
3
```
         5 2
   9 ) 4 6 8
       4 5
         1 8
```
4
```
         8 6
   6 ) 5 1 6
       4 8
         3 6
```

With 198 ÷ 3, 265 ÷ 5, 264 ÷ 4 and 312 ÷ 6 written on, the solutions are:

1
```
         6 6
   3 ) 1 9 8
       1 8
         1 8
```
2
```
         5 3
   5 ) 2 6 5
       2 5
         1 5
```
3
```
         6 6
   4 ) 2 6 4
       2 4
         2 4
```
4
```
         5 2
   6 ) 3 1 2
       3 0
         1 2
```

MD7.3 Choosing how to divide

TB pages 71–72

A1 Children record whether they have solved each division in their head with jottings, as a written short division or using a calculator. Workings should be shown for whichever method they choose.

a 56 ÷ 7 = 8, most likely done in their head

b 424 ÷ 2 = 212, most likely done in their head

c 345 ÷ 5 = 69, most likely done using written short division:

```
      6 9
5 ) 3 4 5
    3 0
    ---
      4 5
```

d 789 ÷ 12 = 65.75, most likely done on a calculator:
press [7][8][9][÷][1][2][=]

e 128 ÷ 4 = 32, most likely done using written short division:

```
      3 2
4 ) 1 2 8
    1 2
    ---
      0 8
```

f 84 ÷ 7 = 12, most likely done in their head or by written short division:

```
      1 2
7 ) 8 4
    7
    ---
    1 4
```

g 396 ÷ 6 = 66, most likely done using written short division:

```
      6 6
6 ) 3 9 6
    3 6
    ---
      3 6
```

h 845 ÷ 15 = 56.3333…, most likely done on a calculator:
press [8][4][5][÷][1][5][=]

i 845 ÷ 50 = 16 r 45 or 16.9, most likely done in their head (16 r 45) or on a calculator:
press [8][4][5][÷][5][0][=]

j 845 ÷ 25 = 33.8, most likely done in their head using the answer to part i (double 16.9) or on a calculator:
press [8][4][5][÷][2][5][=]

B1 a Most likely done in their head:
£1.40 ÷ 20p = 140p ÷ 20p = 7 packets

b Most likely done by written short division:

```
      7 3
8 ) 5 8 4
    5 6
    ---
      2 4
```

584 cm ÷ 8 = 73 cm

c Most likely done on a calculator:
press [2][4][3][1][÷][1][7][=]
£2431 ÷ 17 = £143

d Either in their head or on a calculator:
press [7][5][0][÷][1][5][0][=]
750 ÷ 150 = 5 pieces

C1 Children's own division word problems about IP 12

MD7.4 Short division with remainders: HTU ÷ U (2)

TB pages 73–74

Other reasonable approximations are acceptable in place of those given.

★1 127 ÷ 5 is roughly 100 ÷ 5 = 20

```
      2 5  r 2
5 ) 1 2 7
    1 0
    ---
      2 7
      2 5
      ---
        2
```

Rounding down, she can buy 25 tickets.

★2 163 ÷ 4 is roughly 200 ÷ 5 = 40

```
      4 0  r 3
4 ) 1 6 3
    1 6
    ---
      0 3
```

Rounding up, he needs 41 cages.

★3   265 ÷ 3 is roughly 300 ÷ 3 = 100

```
      8 8 r 1
   3 ) 2 6 5
       2 4
         2 5
         2 4
           1
```

Rounding down, she can make 88 stools.

A1   158 ÷ 7 is roughly 200 ÷ 10 = 20

```
      2 2 r 4
   7 ) 1 5 8
       1 4
         1 8
         1 4
           4
```

Rounding up, she will need 23 pages.

A2   287 ÷ 6 is roughly 300 ÷ 10 = 30

```
      4 7 r 5
   6 ) 2 8 7
       2 4
         4 7
         4 2
           5
```

Rounding down, he can buy 47 chewy bars.

A3   129 ÷ 9 is roughly 150 ÷ 10 = 15

```
      1 4 r 3
   9 ) 1 2 9
       9
         3 9
         3 6
           3
```

Rounding up, the lift must be used at least 15 times.

B1   Probably easiest done on a calculator:
press ③ ⑨ ④ ÷ ① ② =
394 ÷ 12 = 32.8333...
Rounding down, there were 32 bags to sell.

B2   Probably easiest done on a calculator:
press ② ⑦ ⑤ ÷ ① ⑥ =
275 ÷ 16 = 17.1875
Rounding up, 18 groups will be needed.

B3   Probably easiest done on a calculator:
press ⑥ ⑦ ⑤ ÷ ① ⑧ =
675 ÷ 18 = 37.5
Rounding down, there will be 37 bags to sell.

B4   Children's own rounding up/down problems

C1   There are 17 × 12 = 204 eggs in the full boxes.
There are 1–11 eggs in the 18th box.
The largest number of eggs is 204 + 11 = 215.
The smallest number of eggs is 204 + 1 = 205.

C2   15 and 18 are the only numbers between 12 and 20 to divide into 90 exactly. 90 ÷ 15 = 6, 90 ÷ 18 = 5, so there could be 5 or 6 candles in each box.

MD8.1 All sorts of short multiplication 1

TB pages 75–76

★1	a	0.4	b	0.6	c	0.8
★2	a	1.4	b	2.1	c	2.8
A1	a	8	b	0.2	c	8.2
A2	a	10	b	1.5	c	11.5
A3	a	21	b	1.8	c	22.8
A4	a	20	b	2.8	c	22.8
A5	a	40	b	5.6	c	45.6

A6   The answers in A5 are double those in A4.

A7   4.1 × 2 is roughly 4 × 2 which equals 8.
My answer is 8.2, which nearly matches 8, so my answer is probably correct.
2.3 × 5 is roughly 2 × 5 which equals 10.
My answer is 11.5, which nearly matches 10, so my answer is probably correct.
7.6 × 3 is roughly 8 × 3 which equals 24.
My answer is 22.8, which nearly matches 24, so my answer is probably correct.
5.7 × 4 is roughly 6 × 4 which equals 24.
My answer is 22.8, which nearly matches 24, so my answer is probably correct.
5.7 × 8 is roughly 6 × 8 which equals 48.
My answer is 45.6, which nearly matches 48, so my answer is probably correct.

B1 a
```
              T  U . t
5.4 × 3   5×3 =  1  5
          0.4×3 =   1 . 2
                 1  6 . 2
```
5.4 × 3 is about 5 × 3 = 15, so the answer 16.2 is probably correct.

b
```
              T  U . t
3.2 × 7   3×7 =  2  1
          0.2×7 =   1 . 4
                 2  2 . 4
```
3.2 × 7 is about 3 × 7 = 21, so the answer 22.4 is probably correct.

c
```
              T  U . t
1.7 × 8   1×8 =     8
          0.7×8 =   5 . 6
                 1  3 . 6
```
1.7 × 8 is about 2 × 8 = 16, so the answer 13.6 is probably correct.

d
```
              T  U . t
6.9 × 7   6×7 =  4  2
          0.9×7 =   6 . 3
                 4  8 . 3
```
6.9 × 7 is about 7 × 7 = 49, so the answer 48.3 is probably correct.

B2 a
```
              T  U . t
1.6 × 8   1×8 =     8
          0.6×8 =   4 . 8
                 1  2 . 8
```
The fence is 12.8 m long.

b
```
              T  U . t
2.5 × 7   2×7 =  1  4
          0.5×7 =   3 . 5
                 1  7 . 5
```
Fido drinks 17.5 litres of water in a week.

C1 a
```
                 H  T  U . t
24.3 × 4  20×4 =    8  0
          4×4 =     1  6
          0.3×4 =         1 . 2
                    9  7 . 2
```

b
```
                 H  T  U . t
61.7 × 3  60×3 =    1  8  0
          1×3 =           3
          0.7×3 =         2 . 1
                    1  8  5 . 1
```

c
```
                 H  T  U . t
53.4 × 6  50×6 =  3  0  0
          3×6 =      1  8
          0.4×6 =         2 . 4
                  3  2  0 . 4
                     1
```

d
```
                 H  T  U . t
123.4 × 5  100×5 =  5  0  0
           20×5 =   1  0  0
           3×5 =       1  5
           0.4×5 =        2 . 0
                    6  1  7 . 0
```

C2 Children investigate the hardest multiplication they can manage where one of the numbers is a decimal fraction.

MD8.3 Long multiplication

TB pages 77–79

★1 a 2 × 4 = 8, 20 × 4 = 80
    b 3 × 2 = 6, 3 × 20 = 60

★2 a 50 × 3 = 150, 50 × 30 = 1500
    b 6 × 20 = 120, 60 × 20 = 1200

A1 a
```
    ×    10   6
   10   100  60    160
    3    30  18     48
                   208
```

b
```
    ×    20   4
   10   200  40    240
    2    40   8     48
                   288
```

A2 a
```
       43           43
    ×   2        ×  20
       86          860
```

b
```
       62           62
    ×   4        ×  40
      248         2480
```

A3 a
```
       31
    ×  22
      620    31 × 20
       62    31 × 2
      682
```

b
```
       42
    ×  35
     1260    42 × 30
      210    42 × 5
        1
     1470
```

A4 a
×	30	1	
20	600	20	620
2	60	2	62
			682

b
×	40	2	
30	1200	60	1260
5	200	10	210
			1470

c
×	60	7	
40	2400	280	2680
2	120	14	134
			2814

d
×	70	6	
30	2100	180	2280
8	560	48	608
			2888

B1 a 32 × 32 is roughly 30 × 30 = 900.

$$\begin{array}{r} 32 \\ \times\ 32 \\ \hline 960 \\ 64 \\ \hline 1024 \end{array}$$ 32 × 30
 32 × 2

b 54 × 26 is roughly 50 × 30 = 1500.

$$\begin{array}{r} 54 \\ \times\ 26 \\ \hline 1080 \\ 324 \\ \hline 1404 \end{array}$$ 54 × 20
 54 × 6

c 67 × 42 is roughly 70 × 40 = 2800.

$$\begin{array}{r} 67 \\ \times\ 42 \\ \hline 2680 \\ 134 \\ \hline 2814 \end{array}$$ 67 × 40
 67 × 2

d 76 × 38 is roughly 80 × 40 = 3200.

$$\begin{array}{r} 76 \\ \times\ 38 \\ \hline 2280 \\ 608 \\ \hline 2888 \end{array}$$ 76 × 30
 76 × 8

B2 a
×	30	2	
30	900	60	960
2	60	4	64
			1024

b
×	50	4	
20	1000	80	1080
6	300	24	324
			1404

B3 a
$$\begin{array}{r} 37 \\ \times\ 23 \\ \hline 740 \\ 111 \\ \hline 851 \end{array}$$ 37 × 20
 37 × 3

So they pay £851 altogether.

b
$$\begin{array}{r} 36 \\ \times\ 24 \\ \hline 720 \\ 144 \\ \hline 864 \end{array}$$ 36 × 20
 36 × 4

So there are 864 cartons altogether.

B4 Children's own long multiplication word problems

C1 a 35 and 23, 44 and 23, and 44 and 35
   b 44 × 35 = 1540
      44 × 23 = 1012
      44 × 18 = 792
      35 × 23 = 805
      35 × 18 = 630
      23 × 18 = 414
   c Children state whether they found the correct pairs in part a.

C2 a 29 and 28: their product is greater than 800 (812) and they total 57
   b Children repeat part a for a target number other than 800.
      Their pair of numbers should be the square root of the target number, rounded to the integers above and below.

Solving problems

SP1.1 Solving puzzles

TB page 80

B1 a There are 70 ways children could complete the number sentence:
207 + 191 = 398
207 + 291 = 498
...
207 + 791 = 998
217 + 181 = 398
217 + 281 = 498
...
297 + 101 = 398
...

b There are 8 ways children could complete the number sentence:
384 − 69 = 315
384 − 59 = 325
...
384 − 19 = 365
484 − 99 = 385
484 − 89 = 395

c There are 9 ways children could complete the number sentence:
8254 + 18 = 8272
8254 + 28 = 8282
8254 + 38 = 8292
8154 + 48 = 8202
...
8154 + 98 = 8252

d 618 − 491 = 127

Children write 2 rules they used, for example:
Always add units to units, tens to tens, and hundreds to hundreds.
Always subtract units from units, tens from tens, and hundreds from hundreds.
Start with the units. It is then easier to carry across columns.

B2 Children's choice of numbers, for example:
a 17 × 97 = 1649, 93 × 89 = 8277
b 115 × 9 = 1035, 999 × 9 = 8991
c 234 ÷ 6 = 39, 345 ÷ 5 = 69
d 1068 ÷ 12 = 89, 3584 ÷ 64 = 56

B3 a 27 × 8 = 216 or 37 × 8 = 296
b 600 ÷ 4 = 150 or 640 ÷ 4 = 160 or 680 ÷ 4 = 170
c 97 × 20 = 1940
d 327 ÷ 3 = 109 or 357 ÷ 3 = 119 or 387 ÷ 3 = 129

C1 Children investigate multiplying an odd number by an odd number.

CM 48

1 a 672
   + 224
   ‾‾‾‾‾
    896

  b 877
   − 342
   ‾‾‾‾‾
    535

  c 268
   + 534
   ‾‾‾‾‾
    802

  d 683
   − 349
   ‾‾‾‾‾
    334

2 For example
a 63 + 49 = 112
b 900 − 300 = 600
c 345 − 300 = 45
d 12 × 2 = 24
e 12 × 9 = 108

3 a 24 × 2 = 48
b 84 × 2 = 168 or 24 × 7 = 168
c 96 ÷ 3 = 32
d 24 ÷ 3 = 8 or 64 ÷ 8 = 8

4 Children change 1 digit in each sentence and try to solve the new sentences.

Homework suggestion

742 × 9 = 6678
724 × 9 = 6516
472 × 9 = 4248
427 × 9 = 3843
274 × 9 = 2466
247 × 9 = 2223

942 × 7 = 6594
924 × 7 = 6468
492 × 7 = 3444
429 × 7 = 3003
294 × 7 = 2058
249 × 7 = 1743

972 × 4 = 3888
927 × 4 = 3708
792 × 4 = 3168
729 × 4 = 2916
297 × 4 = 1188
279 × 4 = 1116

974 × 2 = 1984
947 × 2 = 1894
794 × 2 = 1588
749 × 2 = 1498
497 × 2 = 994
479 × 2 = 958

SP1.2 Understanding operations

TB pages 81–82

- A1   273 + 319 ≈ 300 + 300 = 600
  273 + 319 = 592
  592 passengers

- A2   394 − 148 ≈ 400 − 150 = 250
  394 − 148 = 246
  246 miles

- A3   8 × 3 ≈ 10 × 3 = 30
  8 × 3 = 24
  24 tyres

- A4   Children's word problem

- B1   5 × 38   5 × 40 = 200
  5 × 38 = 190
  Harry has enough petrol for 190 miles, so he has enough to get back.

- B2   4 + 8 + 2 + 6 = 4 + 6 + 8 + 2 = 20
  20 × £15.50 ≈ 20 × £15 = £300
  20 × £15.50 = £310

- B3   8 × 6 × £12 ≈ 10 × 5 × £10 = £500
  8 × 6 × £12 = £576

- B4   Children's word problem, e.g. Harry gave a lesson to 4 people and was paid £48. How much did each of them pay?

- C1   a   There are 9 possible solutions:
  881 + 719 = 1600,   881 + 729 = 1610,
  881 + 739 = 1620,   881 + 749 = 1630,
  881 + 759 = 1640,   881 + 769 = 1650,
  881 + 779 = 1660,   881 + 789 = 1670,
  881 + 799 = 1680
       b   672 − 409 = 263
       c   162 ÷ 6 = 27

- C2   Children's word problems for the calculations in C1

- C3   Children's word problem

CM 49

1   £4729 − £1843 = £2886

2   8 × 796 km = 6368 km

3   6 kg ÷ 3 = 2 kg
      6 kg + 2 kg = 8 kg

SP1.3 Choosing and using operations

TB pages 83–84

Children should do each calculation in 2 ways.

- A1   49p + 61p + 23p + 77p = 210p or £2.10
  £2 is not enough.

- A2   112p − 63p = 49p
  She bought a Fizzy Wizzy

- A3   244p ÷ 4 = 61p
  He bought 4 Bangers.

- B1   £1.33 + £1.40 + 99p + £1.35 = £5.07
  He got £4.93 change.

- B2   Elspeth spent £1.40 + 99p = £2.39
  Tanya spent £1.33 + £1.35 = £2.68
  Tanya spent 29p more than Elspeth.

- B3   1 of each lolly uses
  62 g + 85 g + 109 g + 74 g = 330 g
  15 of each uses 330 g × 15 = 4950 g
  Larry used 4950 g or 4.950 kg

- C1   Frances spent £5 − 97p = £4.03
  She bought 2 Lucky Dippers and 1 Super Chew.

- C2   Children make up a problem, and solve their partner's problem.

SP2.1 Choosing the best way to multiply

TB page 85

- B1   a   Children's own choice of one number from box 1 (3, 5, 7, 9, 13, 26, 48 or 57) and one from box 2 (4, 6, 8, 10, 11, 40, 212 or 369) that they can multiply mentally. The most sensible choices are 1-digit numbers or 10, e.g. 3 and 4 or 3 and 10. Then they multiply them mentally, e.g. 3 × 4 = 12 or 3 × 10 = 30.
       b   Children repeat part a for another pair of numbers.

- B2   a   Children's own choice of one number from box 1 and one from box 2 that they can multiply using jottings. The most sensible choices are a 1-digit number with a 2-digit number (other than 10 or 40) or a 2-digit number with 40, e.g. 26 and 4 or 13 and 40. Then they multiply them using jottings, e.g. 26 × 4 = 104 or 13 × 40 = 520.
       b   Children repeat part a for another pair of numbers.

B3 a Children's own choice of one number from box 1 and one from box 2 that they can multiply using a standard written method. The most sensible choices are two 2-digit numbers (other than 10 and 40) or a 3-digit number with a 1-digit number, e.g. 26 and 11 or 212 and 5. Then they multiply them using a standard written method, e.g. $26 \times 11 = 272$ or $212 \times 5 = 1060$.
   b Children repeat part a for another pair of numbers.

B4 a Children's own choice of one number from box 1 and one from box 2 that they can multiply using a calculator. The hardest numbers to multiply any other way are probably 57 and 369. Then they multiply them using a calculator, e.g. $57 \times 369 = 21\,033$.
   b Children repeat part a for another pair of numbers.

C1 a In pairs, children make two 2-digit numbers by each throwing 2 dice, e.g. 12 and 56.
   b Each child estimates the product of the numbers in part a, e.g. $10 \times 60 = 600$ and $10 \times 55 = 550$.
   c Children multiply their numbers from part a. The child whose estimate was closest wins a point, e.g. $12 \times 56 = 672$, so the child whose estimate was 10×60 wins a point.
   d Children repeat parts a–c 9 more times to see who wins the most points.

Homework suggestion

You can make exactly 6 different pairs from 4 numbers, which can be multiplied either way round, e.g. 12, 23, 34 and 45 give:
$12 \times 23 = 276$
$12 \times 34 = 408$
$12 \times 45 = 540$
$23 \times 34 = 782$
$23 \times 45 = 1035$
$34 \times 45 = 1530$

SP2.2 Solving word problems

TB pages 86–87

A1 a This can probably be calculated mentally or with jottings, by multiplying 4 lots of 30 and adjusting: $29 + 27 + 33 + 31 = 120 - 1 - 3 + 3 + 1 = 120$ badges
   b $5 + 5 + 6 + 6 = 22$ packs
   c $4 + 2 + 3 + 1 = 10$, enough to make 2 more packs between them.

A2 a $351 - 174 = 177$ more footballs
   b $83 - 37 = 46$ more basketballs

A3 a $7 \times 8 = 56$ netballs
   b 12 boxes ($8 \times 12 = 96$)

B1 a $7 \times 30 = 210$ and $4 \times 45 = 180$, so $210 + 180 = 390$ boxes altogether
   b $11 \times 35 = 385$, so Bill would not be able to store so many boxes.

B2 $478 \div 2 = 239$ marbles in half a box, so he must sell $239 - 126 = 113$ more marbles.

B3 Taking the extra videos sold this week away from the total sold gives double the amount sold last week:
$24 - 6 = 18$
Halving this gives the number sold last week:
$18 \div 2 = 9$ videos

B4 a There are 24 gold ribbons, so there must be 12 blue ribbons. There are $96 - 24 - 12 = 60$ red and green ribbons.
   b $60 \div 3 = 20$, so there are 20 green ribbons and 40 red ribbons. There are $40 - 20 = 20$ more red than green.
   c $40 - 20 = 20$ more green ribbons
$40 - 24 = 16$ more gold ribbons
$40 - 12 = 28$ more blue ribbons

SP2.3 Solving money problems

TB pages 88–89

A1 a £1.19 + £2.89 + 81p = £4.89
   b £5.00 − £4.89 = 11p
   c $3 \times$ (£1.19 + 81p) = $3 \times$ £2 = £6

A2 £12.50 + £9.85 + £5.78 = £28.13

A3 a £54 ÷ 3 = £18
   b £100 − £54 = £46
   c £18 × 2 = £36

B1 a   52 × 20p = £10.40, so Jim can afford either shorts or socks.
    b   £15 + £10.40 = £25.40
        Jim can now afford any of the following combinations:
        2 shirts (£25)
        1 shirt + 1 pair of shorts (£22.35)
        1 shirt + 2 pairs of socks (£24.06)
        1 shirt + 1 pair of socks (£18.28)
        1 shirt (£12.50)
        2 pairs of shorts (£19.70)
        1 pair of shorts + 2 pairs of socks (£21.41)
        1 pair of shorts + 1 pair of socks (£15.63)
        1 pair of shorts (£9.85)
        4 pairs of socks (£23.12)
        3 pairs of socks (£17.34)
        2 pairs of socks (£11.56)
        1 pair of socks (£5.78)

B2 a   Triangular badges cost 28p each, square badges cost 36p each. *37½p*
    b   It is cheapest to buy 10 triangular badges.

B3 There are 13 ways:
    50p + 5 × 20p
    50p + 4 × 20p + 2 × 10p
    50p + 4 × 20p + 10p + 2 × 5p
    50p + 4 × 20p + 10p + 5p + 2p + 3 × 1p
    50p + 4 × 20p + 10p + 5p + 2 × 2p + 1p
    50p + 4 × 20p + 10p + 3 × 2p + 4 × 1p
    50p + 4 × 20p + 2 × 5p + 3 × 2p + 4 × 1p
    50p + 3 × 20p + 3 × 10p + 2 × 5p
    50p + 3 × 20p + 3 × 10p + 5p + 2 × 2p + 1p
    50p + 3 × 20p + 3 × 10p + 5p + 2p + 3 × 1p
    50p + 3 × 20p + 3 × 10p + 3 × 2p + 4 × 1p
    50p + 3 × 20p + 2 × 10p + 2 × 5p + 3 × 2p + 4 × 1p
    5 × 20p + 3 × 10p + 2 × 5p + 3 × 2p + 4 × 1p

C1 Children's own money word problems to match given answers
    a   £34.70   b   £27.90
    c   £12   d   £6.25

CM 50

1   a   £2.20 + £10.30 + £6.40 = £18.90
    b   £20 − £18.90 = £1.10
2   a   £4 × 5 = £20
    b   £4 × 7 = £28
3   a   10 ÷ 5 = 2
    b   20 ÷ 5 = 4

SP2.4 Solving measures problems

TB pages 90–91

A1 a   345 ml + 425 ml = 770 ml
    b   655 ml and 575 ml

A2 2000 ml − 640 ml = 1360 ml

A3 a   6 × 50 litres = 300 litres
        300 000 ÷ 200 = 1500 fans can have a cup of soup
    b   6 × 200 ml = 1200 ml

A4 6 kg ÷ 75 g = 6000 g ÷ 75 g = 80 sandwiches

B1 a   1.5 km + 16 km + 9.5 km = 27 km
    b   42 km − 27 km = 15 km

B2 a   2.5 kg ÷ 500 = 5 g per sheet
        2 × 5 g = 10 g per leaflet
    b   300 × 10 g = 3000 g = 3 kg

B3 a   240 ÷ 12 = 20
        20 × 160 g = 3200 g
        They will need 4 bags of sugar.
    b   160 ÷ 12 = 13.333
        13.333 g for 1 sweet
        13.333 × 16 = 213.333
        213.333 g for 1 bag
        3000 ÷ 213.333 = 14.662
        14 bags

C1 a   13 m ÷ 2.6 m = 5, so Bill can make 5 skipping ropes from each 13 m length. He needs eight 13 m lengths for 36 skipping ropes.
    b   40 skipping ropes

SP3.1 Investigating a general statement

TB page 92

Investigation 1
a   5184   b   7767   c   8622
d   The digit-totals are 18, 27 and 18.
    The digit-totals are all multiples of 9:
    18 = 2 × 9, 27 = 3 × 9, 18 = 2 × 9

Investigation 2
a   Children's own 3-digit multiples of 9. These are best found by multiplying 2-digit numbers by 9, e.g. 17 × 9 = 153, 52 × 9 = 468, 87 × 9 = 783.
b   Yes, the digit-totals are all multiples of 9.

c   Children's own 3-digit numbers whose digits total multiples of 9.
These are most easily found by first picking a multiple of 9 (9, 18 or 27), then finding 3 digits to total it, e.g. 9 = 1 + 2 + 7 so choose 127, 18 = 1 + 9 + 8 so choose 198 and 27 = 9 + 9 + 9 so choose 999.
Any numbers generated in this way will be multiples of 9.

Investigation 3
a   6 + 5 = 11, which is not a multiple of 9
b   Children's own 3-digit numbers whose digits do not total multiples of 9.
The easiest way is to add or subtract 1 from one of the digits in each number in 2c, e.g. 128 (add 1 unit), 298 (add 1 hundred) and 989 (subtract 1 ten).
No, the starting numbers are not multiples of 9.
c   Children's own 4-digit numbers whose digits do not total multiples of 9.
These can be easily generated from the answers to part b by multiplying by 10 or including 9 as an extra digit, e.g. 1280 (128 × 10), 2989 (insert extra 9 in 298) and 9989 (insert extra 9 in 989).
d   No, a number cannot be a multiple of 9 if its digits do not total a multiple of 9.

Investigation 4
a   3, 6, 9, 12, 15, 18, 21, 24, 27, 30, 33, 36
b   3, 6, 9, 3, 6, 9, 3, 6, 9, 3, 6, 9
c   The digit-totals are all multiples of 3. This is true for all multiples of 3.

Homework suggestion

The multiples of 11 are 110, 121, 132, 143, 154, 165, 176, 187 and 198.
The digit-totals are 2, 4, 6, 8, 10, 12, 14, 16 and 18. So, the digit-totals of multiples of 11 are the multiples of 2 in order. However, not all numbers whose digit-totals are multiples of 2 are themselves multiples of 11, e.g. 112.
You can check whether a number between 100 and 200 is a multiple of 11 by checking that the tens digit is one more than the units digit.

SP3.2 Choosing methods

TB pages 93–95

★1 a   2 × 60p = £1.20
    b   10 × 60p = £6
    c   7 × 60p = £4.20
    d   12 × 60p = £7.20

A1   4 × 60p = £2.40

A2   5 × 12 = 60 tables

A3   £456 + £129 + £85 = £670

A4   a   2 × (30 m + 24 m) = 2 × 54 m = 108 m
     b   108 m ÷ 9 m = 12, so 12 strings of lights

B1   145 × 25p = £36.25
     £50 − £36.25 = £13.75 change

B2   2 disco tickets cost £1.20
     £1.20 − 14p = £1.06
     £1.06 ÷ 2 = 53p
     She had 53p in the jar.

B3   a   £150 ÷ 60p = 250, so 250 tickets
     b   £150 − £1.20 = £148.80

B4   25% of £30 = £7.50
     She paid £30 − £7.50 = £22.50

B5   ($13.86 ÷ $1.60) × £1 = £8.66

B6   a   (9 × 7) + 9 = 63 + 9 = 72 slices
     b   11 plates

C1   a   45 minutes = 45 × 60 seconds = 2700 seconds
         2700 ÷ 45 = 60, so 60 tickets
     b   300 ÷ 60 = 5 days

Homework suggestion

4 tickets would cost 4 × 80p = £3.20, 300 would cost 300 × 80p = £240.

SP3.3 Choosing number operations

TB pages 96–97

A1   a   123 × 30p = £36.90
     b   £36.90 − £14.99 = £21.91

A2   20 × 70p = £14

A3   a   £16.50 + £23.75 = £40.25
     b   £16.50 ÷ £1.10 = 15, so 15 hot dogs
         £23.75 ÷ £1.25 = 19, so 19 hamburgers

A4   156 ÷ 4 = 39 jelly babies each

B1 360 − 178 = 182 girls altogether
    182 − 10 = 172 girls on Monday

B2 343 − 138 − 47 = 158 children

B3 18 × 6 = 108, 108 + 3 = 111 sweets originally

B4 125 × 35p = £43.75
    £43.75 − £29.99 = £13.76

B5 (125 × 35p) + (140 × £1.10) + (128 × £1.25)
    + (400 × 70p) = £43.75 + £154 + £160 + £280
    = £637.75

SP3.4 Choosing units

TB pages 98–99

1   250 g + 2 kg + $\frac{1}{4}$ kg = $\frac{1}{4}$ kg + 2 kg + $\frac{1}{4}$ kg =
    $2\frac{1}{2}$ kg or 2.5 kg or 2 kg 500 g

2   750 ml + 185 ml + $1\frac{1}{2}$ l =
    750 ml + 185 ml + 1 l 500 ml = 2 l 435 ml

3   a   1 kg + 300 g + 300 g + 0.1 kg + 300 g +
        0.1 kg = 1 kg + 300 g + 300 g + 100 g +
        300 g + 100 g = 2 kg 100 g or 2.1 kg
    b   500 g mixed fruit
        150 g butter
        150 g flour
        50 g nuts
        150 g sugar
        50 g cherries

4   3 m − 80 cm = 220 cm

5   41 times

6   2.1 m + 11 mm =
    2100 mm + 11 mm = 2111 mm
    Sally can't reach the fairy lights.

7   1.6 km − 790 m = 1600 m − 790 m = 810 m

8   260 km + 12.5 km + 2000 m =
    260 km + 12.5 km + 2 km = 274.5 km

9   They can make 4 from each pack,
    so 12 altogether

10 The whole cake weighed 1050 g.
    75% of 1050 g is 787.5 g, so there is
    1050 g − 787.5 g = 262.5 g left.

Homework suggestion

Large bottles of drink tend to have their capacities given in litres, whilst small bottles/cans have their capacities given in millilitres. Small sachets of sugar are measured in grams, big bags in kilograms. Motorway signs for roadworks are in yards, whilst distances to places are given in miles. Sprint races are measured in metres but long distance races are sometimes measured in miles.

SP3.5 Using written methods

TB page 100

A1 Children's own 3-digit, 2-digit and 1-digit numbers, e.g. 142, 36 and 5
    a   Children add their numbers,
        e.g. 142 + 36 + 5 = 183
    b   Children multiply their largest number by their middle sized number,
        e.g. 142 × 36 = 5112
    c   Children subtract their middle sized number from their largest number,
        e.g. 142 − 36 = 106
    d   Children divide their largest number by their smallest number,
        e.g. 142 ÷ 5 = 28 r 2
    e   Children divide their largest number by their 2-digit number,
        e.g. 142 ÷ 36 = 3 r 34

B1 Children check their answers to A1 using a calculator

B2 Children's own stories to match their calculations in A1

C1 Children repeat A1 and B2 using a 4-digit, a 3-digit and a 2-digit number

SP4.1 Approximate and clear first

TB page 101

1   Including Jeanette there will be 16 at the party.
    a   16 × 35p = 560p or £5.60
    b   4 × 47p = 188p or £1.88
    c   16 × (12p + 7p) = 304p or £3.04
    d   Children's choice of number of packs of streamers at 92p and balloons at 63p to buy
    e   6 × £1.39 = £8.34
        Change £1.66

2   Children's choice of sweets costing no more than £5

3   Children's choice of party supplies costing no more than £20

SP4.2 Reasonable answers

TB pages 102–103

1. estimate: $10 \times 4 = 40$
   answer: $12 \times 4 = 48$
   check: $48 \div 4 = 12$

2. estimate: $6 \times 40 = 240$
   answer: £5.83 × 43 = £250.69
   check: £250.69 ÷ 43 = £5.83

3. estimate: $60 \div 20 = 3$
   answer: 3 minibuses take only 60 people. So you need 4 minibuses.
   check: $4 \times 20 = 80$

A1 For example:
   a Probably quickest mentally:
     2 bookmarks cost £1, so 4 bookmarks cost £2.
   b Probably quickest with a calculator:
     estimate: £2000 − £1950 = £50
     answer: £52.68
     check: £1947.32 + £52.68 = £2000
   c Probably quickest mentally:
     The books cost almost £4, so 2 books cost almost £8, and 3 books cost almost £12. You can buy 2 books for £10.
   d Probably quickest using a calculator:
     estimate: £7 + £6 + £5 + £3 = £21
     answer: £21.68
     check: 21.68 − 3.49 = 18.19,
     18.19 − 4.99 = 13.2, 13.2 − 6.25 = 6.95
   e Probably quickest mentally:
     £5 − 1p + £4.19 = £9.18
     £10 − £9.18 = 82p

B1 a How's Harry: £368.35
     All About Animals: £181.25
     Silly Science: £79.84
     Tales from the Trees: £261.75
   b Total: £891.19
   c They need £491.19 more.

SP4.3 Calculators and brackets

TB page 104

A1 a $56 \times (14 + 19) = 56 \times 33 = 1848$
     $(56 \times 14) + 19 = 784 + 19 = 803$
   b $93 + (71 \times 65) = 93 + 4615 = 4708$
     $(93 + 71) \times 65 = 164 \times 65 = 10\,660$
   c $80 + (120 \div 20) = 80 + 6 = 86$
     $(80 + 120) \div 20 = 200 \div 20 = 10$
   d $43 \times (2088 \div 36) = 43 \times 58 = 2494$
     $(43 \times 2088) \div 36 = 89\,784 \div 36 = 2494$
   e $165 \div (11 + 44) = 165 \div 55 = 3$
     $(165 \div 11) + 44 = 15 + 44 = 59$
   f $256 \div (16 \times 48) = 256 \div 768 = 0.333333$
     $(256 \div 16) \times 48 = 16 \times 48 = 768$

A2 The only two that give the same answer are A1d.

B1 b −4
   c −3, −2, −1, 0

B2 b 9, 7, 5, 3, 1, −1, −3, −5, −7, −9

B3 a $(67 \div 3) \times 9 = \mathbf{201}$
   b $(83 \div 7) \times 14 = \mathbf{166}$

C1 a $56 + 57 + 58 = 171$
   b $63 + 64 + 65 + 66 = 258$

CM 55

1. e 8078   f BLOB
2. Children's calculation with answer 8078
3. Children's calculation with answer 3705 such as $(8000 \div 2) − 300 + 5$
4. Children's calculation with answer 0.7734, such as $((150 \times 50) + 250 − 16) \div 10\,000$

Assessment

AS1 TH page 26
10 pairs are possible:
389 = 152 + 237
898 = 152 + 746
937 = 152 + 785
1022 = 785 + 237
1479 = 694 + 785
846 = 152 + 694
931 = 694 + 237
983 = 746 + 237
1440 = 746 + 694
1531 = 746 + 785

AS2 TH page 26
695 − 376 = 319 DAN
837 − 164 = 673 HID
918 − 378 = 540 GEM
532 − 453 = 79   IN
951 − 108 = 843 RED
712 − 497 = 215 BAG

AS3 TH page 27
7008 − 6997 = 11
5011 − 4993 = 18
8006 − 6992 = 1014
5007 − 1989 = 3018
3002 − 2990 = 12
4005 − 3989 = 16
6012 − 1994 = 4018
9015 − 7992 = 1023

AS4 TH page 27

+	150	280
230	380	510
360	510	640

1325 + 600 = 1925
1325 − 600 = 725

1325 + 400 = 1725
1325 − 400 = 925

874 + 600 = 1474
874 − 600 = 274

874 + 400 = 1274
874 − 400 = 474

AS5 CM 56
1 a 472
  b 843
  c 8231
  d 8367
  e 4586

2 a
```
   7045
    304
  + 516
  -----
   7865
```
  b
```
   6243
     54
  + 371
  -----
   6668
```

3 a Total cost of a laptop, printer and chair is £2379
  b Total cost of a photocopier, filing cabinet and printer is £659

AS6 CM 57
1 a 324   b 3164   c 2082   d 5729

2 a
```
   4638
 − 1295
 ------
   3343
```
  b
```
   3817
 −  476
 ------
   3341
```

3 a 1685 g − 138 g = 1547 g
  b 8829 g − 796 g = 8033 g

AS7 CM 58
1 4.5 and 5.5
  3.7 and 6.3
  0.8 and 9.2

2 a 7.9   b 8.3   c 2.1
  d 8.0   e 11.0 f 3.7

3 a 11.59 b 8.93 c 5.43 d 6.26

4 a
```
   £2.36
 + £7.82
 ------
  £10.18
```
  b
```
   £8.94
 − £3.57
 ------
   £5.37
```

MD1 CM 59
1 a T   b T   c F   d T

2 6 × 48 = 288
  288 ÷ 6 = 48
  288 ÷ 48 = 6

3 a 455 ÷ 7 = 65 or 455 ÷ 65 = 7   T
  b 517 ÷ 11 = 47 or 517 ÷ 47 = 11   T
  c 265 ÷ 5 = 53 or 265 ÷ 53 = 5   T
  d 344 ÷ 18 = 19.111… or 344 ÷ 19 = 18.105… F

4 a 36 × 8 = 288   T
  b 58 × 6 = 348   F
  c 97 × 5 = 485   T
  d 86 × 12 = 1032   T

MD3 CM 60
1 a 3
  b 6
  c $7\frac{2}{4}$ or $7\frac{1}{2}$
  d $3\frac{3}{9}$ or $3\frac{1}{3}$

2 a $7 ÷ 3 = 2\frac{1}{3}$
  b $21 ÷ 5 = 4\frac{1}{5}$
  c $32 ÷ 5 = 6\frac{2}{5}$
  d $15 ÷ 4 = 3\frac{3}{4}$
  e $13 ÷ 2 = 6\frac{1}{2}$
  f $17 ÷ 6 = 2\frac{5}{6}$

3   a $25 \div 7 = 3\frac{4}{7}$
      b $39 \div 6 = 6\frac{3}{6}$ or $6\frac{1}{2}$
      c $52 \div 8 = 6\frac{4}{8}$ or $6\frac{1}{2}$

4    $\frac{1}{4} = 0.25$ $\frac{3}{4} = 0.75$ $\frac{1}{5} = 0.2$ $\frac{1}{10} = 0.1$

5   £2.25

6   a   £1.30   b   £0.52
      c   £0.65   d   £0.26

MD4 TH page 28

24 divisions are possible:

$865 \div 4 = 216$ r 1 $864 \div 5 = 172$ r 4
$856 \div 4 = 214$ $846 \div 5 = 169$ r 1
$685 \div 4 = 171$ r 1 $684 \div 5 = 136$ r 4
$658 \div 4 = 164$ r 2 $648 \div 5 = 129$ r 3
$586 \div 4 = 146$ r 2 $486 \div 5 = 97$ r 1
$568 \div 4 = 142$ $468 \div 5 = 93$ r 3

$854 \div 6 = 142$ r 2 $654 \div 8 = 81$ r 6
$845 \div 6 = 140$ r 5 $645 \div 8 = 80$ r 5
$584 \div 6 = 97$ r 2 $564 \div 8 = 70$ r 4
$548 \div 6 = 91$ r 2 $546 \div 8 = 68$ r 2
$485 \div 6 = 80$ r 5 $465 \div 8 = 58$ r 1
$458 \div 6 = 76$ r 2 $456 \div 8 = 57$

SP1 CM 61

1   a   42 + 27 = **69**   b   93 − **57** = 36
      c   49 + 16 = **65**   d   52 − 35 = **17**
      e   54 + 27 = **81**   f   69 − 21 = **48**

2   Children's own number sentences

3   a   £15 × 8 = £120
         Joe gets £120
      b   £15 × 4 = £60 and £7.50 × 3 = £22.50
         £60 + £22.50 = £82.50
         Joe gets £82.50
      c   3 of the following:
         6 bikes for the whole day
         5 bikes for the whole day and
         2 for half days
         4 bikes for the whole day and
         4 for half days
         3 bikes for the whole day and
         6 for half days
         2 bikes for the whole day and
         8 for half days
         1 bike for the whole day and
         10 for half days
         12 bikes for half days (1 bike can be
         hired out for 2 half days.)

4   Children's own 2-step problem

SP2 CM 62

1   2 CDs and a computer game together cost £33.97, so Phil has £6.03 left to spend on models.
Each model costs just under £3, so he can buy 2.

2   a   Fran puts 120 roses into bunches of 10 (12 × 10 = 120).
         This leaves 80 roses to put into bunches of 6.
         $80 \div 6 = 13$ r 2 (or $13\frac{2}{6}$ or 13.333...), so there will be 13 bunches of 6, with 2 roses left over.
      b   The 200 roses must be divided into 2 groups as follows: the number of roses in the group to be put into bunches of 6 must be a multiple of 6 and of 10 (30 or 60 or 90 or 120 or 150 or 180).
      c   £6.49 × 7 = £45.43
         £3.99 × 5 = £19.95
         £45.43 + £19.95 = £65.38 (total cost)

SP3 TH page 29

The table below shows what to divide by and what to subtract to get back to the start number, according to how many consecutive numbers have been chosen.

How many consecutive numbers?	Divide by	Subtract
1	1	0
2	2	0.5
3	3	1
4	4	1.5
5	5	2
6	6	2.5
7	7	3
8	8	3.5
9	9	4
10	10	4.5

SP4 TH page 29

Adding 91, hundreds and units digits increase by 1 each time. Tens digit decreases by 1 each time.

    91
  182
  273
  364
  455
  546
  637
  728
  819
  910

Adding 98, units digit decreases by 2 each time. Hundreds digit increases by 1 each time. Tens digit remains constant for a block of 5 numbers, then decreases by 1.

    98
  196
  294
  392
  490
  588
  686
  784
  882
  980
1078
1176
1274
1372
1470
1568
1666
1764
1862
1960
2058